# Goodbye to God

## Searching for a *Human* Spirituality

## Chris Scott

Cover design by Spiffing Covers Ltd.

Paperback ISBN – 978-1-910667-20-0
Mobi ISBN – 978-1-910667-21-7
ePub ISBN – 978-1-910667-22-4

This book is dedicated to the memory of Steven Weddle. Scourge of religiosity, pomposity and pretentiousness, he lived out what this book tries to convey. You are greatly missed Steve.

# Acknowledgements

I say in this book that the spiritual journey is not something to be undertaken alone. For more than thirty years Ruth has not only been my wife, but my soul mate and so very often, my inspiration. In many ways there is much of her in this book, for which I am deeply grateful.

Many other people too have played a part in the writing and publication of this book. A number in particular deserve my special thanks: Jenny Zarek and Sue Sabbagh laboured generously and productively on my initial dyslexic manuscripts, helping to make them readable. Thank you.

Others encouraged me to commit my thoughts to paper, through their personal support and the inspiration I drew from reading their words. One especially, the late Michael Nevin, inspired me to be adventurous in my thinking. For his support and witty theological and philosophical teaching, I shall always be grateful.

I am particularly indebted to my editor and good friend John Lilley. His good-humoured encouragement, and expertise in pulling the text together in a more coherent form, made the editing process a delight not a chore.

All biblical quotations are taken from The New Oxford Bible, New Revised Standard Version 1991. Other quotations used are acknowledged within the text or are referenced.

*This be the Verse* is from 'The Complete Poems Of Philip Larkin' by Philip Larkin, edited by Archie Burnett. Copyright © 2012 by The Estate of Philip Larkin. Reprinted by permission of Farrar, Straus and Giroux, LLC, in the United States, and Faber & Faber Ltd, Bloomsbury House, 74-77 Great Russell Street, London WC1B 3DA in the United Kingdom.

# Contents

# FOREWORD

When my friend Chris Scott invited me to write the Foreword to *Goodbye to God*, I felt two things at once: honored and challenged. Honoured because Chris is a man for whom I have great esteem; challenged because bidding farewell to God is not on my bucket list. It was a dilemma until I began reading and realised to my relief that my friendship and my faith were not at odds. *Goodbye to God* is, I discovered, a book challenging its readers not to faith, nor to doubt, nor to disbelief, but to honesty and freedom. The spirituality it sets before us and dares us to pursue 'transcends religions, beliefs, dogmas, creeds, scientific proofs, scepticism and polarity'. Its pages are meant to bring together, off the street as it were, anyone and everyone without a spiritual home and yet alive with longing for a spiritual life.

Spiritual unity may seem an oxymoron. We humans, though sharing a common spiritual thirst, mostly drink from our own private wells we have dug, often gated and proprietary, open to us, closed to others. Institutional religion is, and appears always, to have been segregated and tribal, dividing believers from non-believers, orthodox from heterodox, observant from non-observant, circumcised from uncircumcised, even man from woman. As I see it, one of Chris Scott's core aims in *Goodbye to God* is to remove, at least for now, the walls and pews, the altars and pulpits, the revelations and rituals, of organised religion so that we might meet as one, as souls in search of life and truth, a life and truth in which we commune rather than contend. 'The spiritual journey,' he writes, 'cannot be taken alone.'

Why, we may wonder, bid farewell to God when it may be God whom we are seeking? Let's be more clear and careful here. Saying goodbye to God doesn't mean God is going to leave. It just means that we humans are going to try to think and feel, imagine and hope, speak and listen as one, to each other, in a gathering and space without incense or altars, scriptures or creeds, doctrines or rituals; without priests, mullahs, rabbis or popes. Call it an experiment, an experiment in simplicity and truth. Here, in these pages, is an 'ecclesia', a church, in which agnostics and atheists are welcome, not to be proselytized and converted, but rather to be acknowledged in their humanity and in their hunger, our human hunger, for a full life. This is, for the record, what Christianity, for one, is supposed to be all about. 'I came that they may have life and have it abundantly.' [John 14:2]

What this book seeks, and succeeds in summoning, is 'a meeting place where peoples of different religious understandings, or none, can come together and share a common understanding of their humanity. This does not mean that a Christian needs to deny his belief, or that a Buddhist needs to change her path, or that an agnostic has to turn believer.' The call to prayer here is 'for all people, of all faiths and none' to 'journey inwards… and there to recognise the oneness of all humanity'.

This journey is nothing more or less than the human journey, at once towards death and life. Even as we are carried along, willing or not, towards extinction, we sense at our core that it remains for us, like salmon, to defy the current, to return to our beginnings, to reach out for fullness even as we are diminished. This is the work of a lifetime and is not over until we are. 'The backward pupil in a school,' wrote Søren Kierkegaard:

> is usually known by his habit of coming forward with his paper scarcely ten minutes after the task has been set, announcing that he has finished it – which must be tiresome for the teacher.… So also… it must be tiresome for the power that governs the world… to have to do with people who have finished the tasks of life almost as soon as they are set.

So what are these 'tasks of life'? Where does the journey we are on take us if we set ourselves to it? Nietzsche, in *Thus Spake Zarathustra*, suggests that we must undergo three metamorphoses along life's way, each with its work to do, each with its own image: the camel, the lion, and the child.

The camel is a beast of burden, and like the camel we bend the knee and accept the load we are given: the truths, the customs, the beliefs, the rituals, the gods or anti-gods, the duties and absolutes of those who hold our reins and lead us in their footsteps. Life is all about change, however, and so the time comes to discover and release the lion in us, to throw off our burdens, to interrogate our truths, to break ranks, refuse commands, and to say goodbye to the god we have carried on our backs and confessed by rote. 'Our first task,' wrote Thomas Merton, 'is to be fully human… There is no need for a community of religious robots without minds, without hearts, without ideas, and without faces.' The lion is not about to be saddled or yoked. As lions, our craving is for freedom, independence, autonomy, and we are willing to fight for it. But this fight is not for ever. It remains for us to take up our final task – the last stage in our becoming – and to be a child. 'Truly I tell you, unless you change and become like little children, you will never enter the kingdom of heaven.' [Matthew 18:13] Surely this is a new childhood that awaits us – unburdened, free, and willing to utter a full and holy 'Yes' to life. Not there yet myself, I am uncertain what that 'yes' will sound like. For now I think of the final childlike words of Dylan Thomas's charming ode to Christmas: 'I said some words to the close and holy darkness, and then I slept.'

Life, then, is arguably all about change and so is the task of living it fully. There is no such thing as standing still. Staying put means losing ground. We have a journey to make, and like the caterpillar, we have metamorphosis in our future. The camel, the lion, and the child suggest the sequence and shape of the changes we will undergo. Unless I have misread *Goodbye to God* and badly mistaken its point, these archetypes – the camel, the lion, and the child – also inhabit the book that Chris Scott has given us. At the least they have been helpful to me, and may prove useful to you, in interpreting the essential challenge the author has put to us his readers. Ultimately it comes down to childhood, the early childhood that we leave behind and the new childhood that we strain to embody. The camel's legs and back eventually give out, and the lion, however loud and fierce, eventually lies down with the lamb. His reign is transitional, not final. Everything, it seems, points to the child as the final fruit of human becoming. Purity of heart, wrote Kierkegaard, is to will one thing; and the one thing with which Chris Scott leaves us is love. 'In the end,' he says, 'it is simplicity itself.' 'In the final analysis,' he writes, 'I believe we are called on to love.... So here we are, drawing our thoughts to a close. I feel that my entire argument could be neatly summarised as: Be loving and practice kindness – but with backbone... That is the essence of the spiritual life, the essence of what it is to be truly human. We need make it no more complicated than that.'

I, too, should perhaps leave it at that; but I am oddly drawn back to the 'backbone' that Chris says must accompany love. I ask myself what he might mean here; and, since I agree with him, I also ask myself what I might mean by it. What I come up with is that the metamorphoses we undergo, the stages we pass through, are messier than we might think or wish. The lion in us retains something of the camel and the child retains something of both, and for good reason, because the truth is that love is never simple, at least not the love whose praise Paul sings in his first letter to the Corinthians. That kind of love is hard going and often requires that we blindly believe in it, carry it with all the dutiful subservience of the camel, and at the same time with the ferocity of the lion, even as we reach beyond faith and duty to embody the loving simplicity of a child.

As I wrote the above I had someone in mind – a woman of profound faith, a lion to her last breath, and a font of love from which countless abandoned souls drank. This was Dorothy Day, the founder of the Catholic Worker Movement, who gave her life, her all, to sheltering, feeding, championing, and befriending – in a word, loving – those whom everyone else, it seemed, had written off. And yet we find this written in her journal:

> The burdens get too heavy; there are too many of them; my love is too small: I even feel with terror, 'I have no love in my heart, I have nothing to give....' And yet I have to pretend that I have. Most strange and wonderful, the make-believe becomes true. If you will to love someone, you soon do. You will to love this cranky old man and someday you do. It depends on how hard you try.

So, it seems, there is always room and need for make-believe, for faith. Not the make-believe of the child, but that of the lion who is losing heart, or the lover who has run dry. This, I suspect, is what Chris has so wisely called 'backbone'.

This book is for camels and lions and the struggling child in us. No matter where you find yourself in what Kierkegaard called 'the stages on life's way', there is something here in this book for you – challenge, charm, heart, humour, courage, understanding, insight, reassurance, companionship. It is a gift for which I thank the author.

Robert Emmet Meagher
Professor of Humanities
Hampshire College
Amherst, Massachusetts.

*And all must love the human form,*
*In heathen, Turk, or Jew;*
*Where Mercy, Love, and Pity dwell*
*There God is dwelling too.*

- William Blake

# PART ONE

# INTRODUCTION

As recently as 100 years ago, belief that the Bible narrative was literally true was widely, if not universally, accepted, and the creeds and doctrines of the Church were rarely questioned. Today, however, while many acknowledge a spiritual dimension to their lives, they find that the institutional religions mostly fail to satisfy their needs. The gap between the questions they ask and the answers the Church or other established religions provide, continues to widen as the hunger for real meaning in life strengthens.

In 1963, John Robinson's challenging book *Honest to God* caused quite a stir. He gave the traditionalists fresh concern by opening up debate about the nature of biblical literature, suggesting that the truth had many more facets to it than a literal or historical reading of the Bible could bear. Certainly, some progressive theological colleges and universities were also insisting that literal interpretations should no longer be accepted without question, but compliant congregations and most clergymen continued to take the Bible at face value.

And that's why the Church could resist Robinson's challenge and generally continue to plough the same old furrow, seemingly oblivious as the world moved on around it. And move on it has – the rise in popularity of the Sunday Assemblies, 'Atheist Churches' as they're sometimes called, suggests that people haven't turned their backs on spirituality, merely on organised religion.

That's why I have written this book. It's for people like me, and you too perhaps, people who believe that the creeds, doctrines and scriptural interpretations of a bygone age will no longer do. I want to explore the possibilities of an alternative understanding of the traditional message, rather than simply exchange one set of rigid doctrines for another. So I'm writing for fringe agnostics as well as committed atheists – that vast swathe of people who sit uncomfortably at the edge of the religion they've been brought up with, or beyond the edge, yet hope to affirm there's more to life than the merely material. In the second half I will use the 'life stories' of the *man* Jesus of Nazareth to show that within these stories lies the heart of what it means to be truly *human,* because that *man* Jesus does, I believe, resonate fully with our own 21ˢᵗ-century experience.

Writing as a Christian priest, I know that many of my fellow Christians will disagree profoundly with the line I am taking and even think me heretical. Yet I feel compelled to write as I do because I believe that the fundamental insights offered by *all* the great religions primarily confirm what it is to be fully *human* and not merely religious. Expressions of religious dogma must, by their very nature, narrow and confine our thinking into manageable units. In the words of Parson Thwackum in Henry Fielding's novel *Tom Jones*: 'When I mention religion I mean the Christian religion, and not only the Christian religion, but the Protestant religion; and not only the Protestant religion, but the Church of England.'

The line between practical boundaries on one side and cementing bigotry and exclusiveness on the other, is a fine one. Yet it is often crossed. Not only does each religion claim a monopoly on eternal values, but every sect and denomination within each religion, claims primacy for its own brand of 'the truth'.

I want to affirm that, quite naturally, human beings embody what the Christian Church calls 'the grace of God', and that it takes no supernatural intervention for people to live their lives to the full. Religion is not an essential component of a good and fulfilled life; on the contrary, it can be life-denying and limiting, the opposite of all it proclaims to be indispensable and true.

What I am suggesting is the possibility of 'secular spirituality'. That may seem contradictory, but only if one ties the idea of spirituality to a conventional religious belief system. I want us to unshackle ourselves from religious notions that no longer speak to women and men in the 21st century. The very word 'god' – in its differing forms central to most religions – is loaded with associations that can, in the very nature of things, have little or nothing to do with the reality it claims to represent.

Secular spirituality is a way of being that may or may not include religious belief; neither its absence nor its inclusion is crucial. What matters is perception and attitude. Although the words 'spirit' and 'spiritual' are loaded with religious connotations, I have retained them for two reasons. One is that I simply cannot think of a better alternative (I'll try to be honest in this book, if nothing else), and, secondly, it is quite possible to strip 'spirit' of its religious overtones. One might speak of the 'spirit of England' or the 'spirit of France', and who would deny that the spirit of each is quite different? Or that the spirit in which sport is played is something not easily defined but almost tangible to those who experience it? In short, experience plays a crucial part in spirituality. For instance, if someone were to talk to me about, say, the 'spirit of the mining community', I couldn't enter confidently into that mood having no first-hand knowledge, so I'd have to rely on unsatisfactory secondhand perceptions.

Secular spirituality is concerned with affirming people's understanding of where they are and what they experience. In detail we all live very different lives, but we share our humanity, our common beginnings and endings – in death we are all united.

I suspect that the way I handle material might attract the wrath of theologians and psychologists alike, but this is no text book, nor is it a religious tract. My ambition is not to pin down technical detail or contextual accuracy. Rather, the 'spirit' of this book will be found in its attempt to make connections at the human and humane levels, to reach beyond the technicalities and divisions of different disciplines and locate common ground in the human spirit. It's this essential part of our humanity which cannot be contained within, or limited by, particular religious doctrines, or yield its nature to scientific or psychological analysis alone. If I appear to be cavalier with the material I use, it's because I have come to believe that the 'objective' nature of both science and religion is as likely to conceal the nature of the human spirit as it is to reveal it. Both are valuable tools and should be treated with honesty and respect, but neither should be credited with 'god'-like status, because if they are, we diminish our true nature and live secondhand lives.

If you have stayed with me this far, you may already have decided that you expect to love this book, or hate it, or ignore it or perhaps suspend your judgement. Whichever way you're inclining will depend upon your perceptions, a thought that leads us nicely into the first chapter.

# CHAPTER 1

## Seeing is believing

Seeing is believing, we're usually told. But years ago, on a visit to the Natural History Museum, I was invited to watch a video of a street scene – a mugging, I believe it was. Then, via a touch-response screen, I was asked to act as a witness, confident about what I thought I'd seen only to learn later, to my horror, that I'd got it completely wrong. If I'd been a real witness I would have testified against the wrong person, although the viewing and my response were only minutes apart. So what happened? Well, I do know that I'm not a very sensing person – that is, I can easily miss seeing or noticing something that others will readily recall. But that wasn't the whole story.

We may like to think we see the world as it is, as an objective reality, and that our eyes and brains merely act as sophisticated recording agents, registering events without distortion and offering instant and accurate play-back. The truth, however, as the philosopher Immanuel Kant put it, is that 'We see the world not as it is, but as we are.' Studies of perception within psychology have shown us that we *create* reality rather than simply observe it. Take the following example. Does the facing picture mean anything to you? Or is it just a mass of blobs and spots?[1]

---

[1] Gregory R (1970) The Intelligent Eye,  Photo: RC James

If I tell you that it's a picture of a Dalmatian dog in the snow, does that help? Perhaps not. If it's driving you to distraction, go to the end of this chapter where things are made a little clearer. Once you've seen the dog, it's almost impossible not to see it. Our perception 'draws in' the outline, projecting meaning onto an otherwise random collection of blobs.

Many years ago, while on a first-aid course, I heard about a girl who'd had a serious cycling accident. She was lying unconscious and bleeding profusely from a wound in the upper leg. A man experienced in first-aid was staunching the flow of blood by applying pressure to the femoral artery. A woman passer-by then 'saw' what he was doing and also went to the girl's assistance, but did so by attacking the man with her umbrella. What she 'saw' was an accident victim being sexually assaulted. She had built her own reality from a mix of visual stimulus and her own experience and expectation.

Now look at the figure below. What do you see?

Can you see the white triangle lying over three black circles and a black triangle? You can? Well done, you have just been creative. In reality there is no white or black triangle; your perception has created them from what your eyes sense and from what you *already know* about shapes and angles. The triangles are mental constructs built on previous experience. Ask a small child what he or she sees and they will describe only the partial black circles – or may use other words based on their own experience, so a partial circle becomes a 'munching mouth'. Such shapes have also been shown to adults from different cultures whose lives involved few angles or straight lines, such as African bushmen. Again, like the children, they will describe what they see in different terms, and the triangle won't be apparent to them because it isn't part of their frame of reference.

My wife, Ruth, is something of a magician. Although she keeps most of her techniques secret even from me, she has let me into a few tricks of the trade – and has plenty of them. But she won't perform some tricks because she believes they're so obvious that everyone will spot them, which is how she reacts when they're done by others, thanks to her prior knowledge. Her perception (that a trick is obvious) stops her performing it and limits her repertoire. Her knowledge informs her perception, and her perception affects her actions.

By now you may be wondering why I'm setting out my stall by focusing on the idiosyncrasies of perception, and why it is a creative process rather than simply a sense-recording system. Yet I hope that by the time you finish this chapter I will have convinced you that truth and reality are not simply 'objects out there' on which we have to focus, but that each individual in effect creates his or her own truth and reality from a combination of external sensory data and internal experiential knowledge.

Given that no two individuals have exactly the same life experience, it follows that there is no such thing as absolutely objective reality or truth unless we're talking about a tautology (to call a circle round is a tautology). In other words it is true to say that a circle is round – because that is the definition of a circle – and if it isn't round, it isn't a circle. So, self-authenticating definitions aside, let us accept that our reality won't necessarily match another person's reality. Even when we're observing the same physical object or event, our own perceptual processes are likely to place a unique slant on what we term 'reality'. And if that is so for the everyday world of material objects, events and encounters, how much more must it be so for the realm of the spiritual?

Some of you will be wondering about the subjectivity of my own outlook. Am I saying that every individual must decide for himself or herself what is true or real? Certainly I believe this is part of the truth, but only a part – there's an interaction between people that isn't objective reality in itself, but nevertheless forms the basis of our communication. Somewhere between the personal (unique and subjective) and the universal (common and objective) lies the Spirit of Humanity.

It is my contention that true spirituality is concerned with this aspect of life, and is common to all people. It emerges from the interface between disciplines that are often considered to be in opposition – for example, science and religion. As popularly conceived, science represents a totally objective, fact-oriented view of life that disregards and eliminates (as if it could) all subjective influences. Equally, religion is regarded as dealing with the 'other-worldly', as having a view of creation that often flies in the face of advancing scientific knowledge, and that tries to speak authoritatively about a supernatural Being.

Such a split between science and religion is false. They represent not different realities, but different perceptions of the same reality.

Let's take an everyday example. A couple inspect a new front door at a DIY store. The man says, 'It's too heavy.' But his wife says, 'No, it's just right, I really like it.' Both are convinced in their view and there's an argument. Who is right? Well, both are, but they disagree because they're talking at cross-purposes. When the man says it's too heavy, he means that the door is too big and weighty, physically, for the hinge mountings and door frame. His wife, on the other hand, is speaking visually – she likes the design and colour of the wood. He can be said to represent the 'scientific' view, and she the 'religious' or, less grandly, the aesthetic.

They are discussing the same reality while encountering problems of both perception and language. Each is concerned with different aspects of the one reality, ie the door, but because each is preoccupied with their own particular concern, neither hears what the other is saying. Both are telling the truth, but it's a partial truth. And therein, even in this banal example, lies the essence of one of the greatest blocks to human fulfilment and happiness.

It is possible to hold differing views and opinions on any subject, of course, both because we bring our own unique perceptions to the debate and because we may be applying quite different criteria to the same reality. As a counsellor and therapist, I have spent a lot of time with couples who worry that their relationship is on the rocks. Time and time again I find that one of their major problems is rooted in clashes of perception and perspective. Not only does each partner have a unique perception, but each is often focusing on different and limited aspects of the same reality. There probably won't be a single reader who has not experienced first-hand the destructive forces that emerge from such crossed wires when communication simply hasn't been possible. So often we assume that our reality is the same as everyone else's, and we become angry and upset or feel rejected and afraid when what is real for us is denied by others.

In fact, the polarisation of beliefs, views, perceptions and interpretations is what can divide humanity, in severe cases highly destructively. In minor forms it may cause trivial upset and irritation, but at its most extreme, it can result in injury, death, warfare and terrorism. A spiritual way of life is, I believe, an alternative way of living creatively between polar opposites. This is where the human race's split personality can become whole, because a spiritual view of life recognises in the heart of the other, a reflection, albeit a very different one, of the self. Unlike particular religious denominations or science which demand a conformity of view from their followers, the spiritual path calls for no conformity and welcomes diversity. It discovers aspects of the truth in the most unlikely (to the individual) places, and is open to the probability that 'my' truth is only partial, and may well need to change in the light of further exploration. The spiritual path won't appeal to those who want certainty and security, but it will to those who wish to live their lives more creatively, where truth becomes an ever-moving and ever-expanding concept.

# CHAPTER 2

## Living the dichotomy

In Chapter 1 I spoke of the area between the subjective and objective as the place where the spirit of humanity thrives. It's a 'touching place' where mutuality and understanding recognise each other and share experiences of love, beauty, tenderness and empathy. It's where two or more people discover a unity of spirit. But before we skip down the path to happy-clappyland where all is warmth and light, let us also acknowledge the dark side. The human spirit of which I speak, the place between the poles, has great destructive as well as creative potential, where you will also find mutuality in hatred, violence, cruelty and greed. While we may unite behind great and truly humanitarian causes, equally we may unite in monstrous endeavour. The collective evil of the Nazi regime was an extreme expression of this dark side. But, alas, we do not need to reach back into history to find such depravity – a glance at any daily newspaper or television news programme reveals only too clearly the depths to which the human spirit can sink.

While acknowledging such destructive potential, however, in this book I wish to explore humanity's positive potential, the spirituality that transcends religions, beliefs, dogmas, creeds, scientific proofs, scepticism and polarity. For simplicity's sake, and to avoid any linguistic misunderstandings, when I use the term 'spiritual' or 'spirituality' in the text I will, from now on, be referring to the positive, life-affirming aspects of the human spirit rather than the destructive side.

But first let me try to define what I mean by the area between the subjective and the objective, this 'living the dichotomy'. There's no word for it in English, and not being a linguist I don't know whether other cultures can offer a helpful description. If they can, I'm sure I'll get to hear about it. Meanwhile, let's define 'living the dichotomy' thus:

> An area of experience that is at one level unique to the individual, inasmuch as it has no empirically provable reference point (subjective); at the same time this experience is held in common with others and appears to have an external source of being (objective).

Put more simply: an experience shared is often perceived as having a source outside itself. And here is the crunch question: is this experience real? Well, certainly it is for each of the individuals concerned, but is it more than merely a collective illusion? An experience common to humanity in general is that of love, an 'affect' that isn't amenable to scientific proof, yet those who share it know that it's real. And sometimes it's equally obvious to outside observers who can see that love is a reality within a particular relationship. So what is going on?

It's this area of common experience that is most easily understood through love that I'm trying to get at. It is neither completely subjective nor unique to one individual, nor is it objective, an 'out there fact' for all to see. It nestles between the two, almost impossible to express (you can see how I'm struggling), yet is common to all humanity. It is, I believe, the very spirit of what it means to be human.

Humanity is often defined in rather concrete terms: we're reasoning and thinking creatures, able to communicate in writing and speech, and able to transcend time through memory and imagination. All such abilities can to a large extent be measured and tested. Yet surely there is also a fifth dimension, a spiritual integration that most individuals feel in their bones to be a reality, even if they're unable to put a name to it, or it conflicts with their scientific viewpoint.

This meeting point of life's dichotomies has of course not gone unrecognised in the past; it is simply that particular groups have claimed it as their own. It might be called the 'soul', the 'spirit of God', or the 'psyche'. The problem is that each group starts with its own perceptions, but goes on to describe this universally human phenomenon in a language that is exclusive unto itself, alienating those who do not share the same starting point. By labelling or describing this centre point, the centre is automatically thrown out of balance and drawn to one pole or the other. Either a religious connotation will be attached, along with the baggage of that particular religion, or scientific explanations will be offered which deny the experience of many millions of people. We struggle therefore with perceptions, language and definition, not of *different* realities, but different understanding of the *same* reality. Attempts to understand and communicate the very essence of our human nature therefore become yet another tool for prising us apart.

This phenomenon, common to human experience and lying between subjectivity and objectivity, I call: ***cojectivity***. If individuals and groups are willing to suspend their claims to exclusivity, then cojectivity can become the meeting place where peoples of different religious understandings, or none, can come together and share a common understanding of their humanity. This does not mean that a Christian needs to deny his belief, or that a Buddhist needs to change her path, or that an agnostic has to turn believer. Through cojectivity we can all accept a common human spirit and spiritual path, but allow each person, through their own perceptions, to find their own way to express it. Such an approach encourages not only greater respect and tolerance for different faith groups, but also for those who wish to express the essentially spiritual nature of their being in secular or humanist terms.

Cojectivity recognises that as human beings we enjoy a potential for creative and positive living that isn't limited to individuals. Nor is it the property of particular faiths or interest groups, but is buried deep in our essential humanity. Cojectivity is the 'touching place' I mentioned earlier, where humanity meets humanity beyond the reach of the systems and parameters we build for ourselves. It is a point where the individual breaks the bonds of his or her individual perception to grasp a vision of what is possible.

I'm finding this chapter is starting to feel a little heavy and dense, so let's lighten it with a story.

Some years ago, when I was a curate (assistant priest) in a Shropshire town, my wife received some visitors while I was out. They were two women, Jehovah's Witnesses, probably in their early thirties. Ruth invited them in, and what followed was a long discussion about the nature of the Bible, belief, faith and the 'life to come'. When I returned home, their conversation had been in progress for well over an hour, but neither Ruth nor our visitors were any nearer to seeing the other's points of view. I then joined in the rhetoric (for that is what it was, neither side really listening to the other), and on we went for a further period of time.

As the morning wore on, Ruth excused herself and went into the kitchen to get on with clearing up after breakfast. One of the two women joined her, picked up a tea towel and started to help. Talk of theology and religion stopped and they began to speak about more personal things. At that time, Ruth was working as a counsellor in a doctors' practice, and had not long before qualified as a midwife. As the conversation progressed, our visitor revealed that she had recently suffered a stillbirth and was still in the process of grieving. Because Ruth herself had suffered a miscarriage and had been trained in midwifery and counselling, heart now met heart. All the earlier debate and arguments about doctrine and belief seemed as irrelevant as yesterday's weather forecast.

What had been happening in the long discussion was that each person's subjective belief had been presented as objective truth. Now, in a meeting of pain and understanding, the shedding of tears and letting go of barriers, each human spirit was able to meet and to recognise and love the other. This is cojectivity, that universally recognisable moment when we move beyond the confines of our own limited experience, without at the same time moving into the realms of material fact or empirical proof.

The most profound and meaningful moments of our lives are cojective. They are experiences we hold in common with other human beings, although they can often only be expressed through poetry, song, art, music, myth or symbol. Sometimes the cojective experience is most powerfully experienced, not through any form of external communication, but in silence. Moments of love, joy, grief or sorrow are felt directly – heart to heart. We know them to be real, to be the most important events in people's lives, yet there is nothing about them that could be labelled objective or factual.

This hinterland of cojectivity, which we all experience yet which seems to defy our attempts to pin it down objectively, is the essence of our humanity, and the subject of this book. It is the most real thing

29

in the world yet, of itself and on its own, it does not exist. It is the go-between that unites human existence and gives it the potential for both quasi-divine goodness and demonic badness.

The wonderful little story by Margery Williams called *The Velveteen Rabbit* illustrates the cojective at work.

> 'What is REAL,' asked the rabbit one day... 'does it mean having things that buzz inside you and a stick-out handle?' 'Real isn't how you are made,' said the Skin Horse. 'It's a thing that happens to you. When a child loves you for a long, long time, not just to play with, but REALLY loves you, then you become Real.'

Like all great fairy stories, *The Velveteen Rabbit* is telling your story and mine. 'Real' is not to be found in the objective, 'things that buzz and have a stick-out handle', nor in the subjective, 'just being played with', but in the interaction *between* human beings. We are most 'real' when we are 'living the dichotomy'. It is a grey area full of risk and potential, danger and fulfilment. It is where the Human Spirit dwells and flows and meets, and it goes by many names.

# CHAPTER 3

## What's in a name?

When our daughter Freya was five, one of her most frequent questions, familiar to most parents of children of that age, was 'Why?' Sure, it's a joy to have a curious child, but satisfying those constant 'whys' can become tricky. When we told Freya the names of things, for example, and she asked, 'Why is it called that?' sometimes there was an easy answer. But sometimes we had to respond, 'Well, that's just what it's called.'

Giving something or someone a name is vital shorthand, making for conversational fluency. Imagine making the following statement – 'I placed the cup and saucer on the table' – without using the familiar labels, but simply relying on descriptive terms. Let's give it a try: 'I placed the china container, which was round at the top, about three inches in diameter and tapering unevenly to two inches at the bottom, and its matching curved and circular china base of about five inches in diameter, on the flat rectangular wooden surface held about three feet above the floor by four vertical wooden…' I'm sure you get the picture.

Denied commonly accepted shorthand terms, conversations would become impossible. Or, at least, we'd be obliged to go into huge detail about very little. So we use names, but in so doing we assume a great deal about the other person's knowledge of the subject, and we implicitly expect the listener to fill in much of the detail. And in everyday matters – the teacup and saucer – the detail is usually irrelevant and does not detract from our understanding and communication.

However, misunderstandings can occur, even with commonplace names, especially when a single term serves more than one purpose.

Many years ago I used to help out at a hospital unit based at the famous Scout Camp, Gilwell Park. One small boy who required more medical attention than we could give him was taken to see a doctor. It has to be said that this particular doctor did not have a way with small children. Looking over his spectacles, he asked the nervous child, 'How are your stools?' The bewildered boy stammered, 'P-Please, sir, I 'aven't got none.' If the doctor had had the wit to ask 'How's your poo?' he would have received the answer he needed.

America and Britain have been described as 'two countries separated by the same language'. English is supposedly common to both, yet both countries have different labels for many commonplace objects: sidewalk/pavement, check/bill, drugstore/chemist and so on. This is also true in many regions of the same country. Local dialect can sometimes make communication very difficult. Not only items, but actions can be given different names, not least when slang is used.

In short, in naming something, some person or action, we use conversational shorthand, but in so doing must accept that there is an inevitable lack of precision. We take it for granted that the other person has a similar frame of reference, and most of the time we have little problem understanding each other. But when subjects become more specialised, greater care needs to be taken to ensure the accuracy of our communication. And when actions are being described, yet more care is needed as we move out of the realm of the concrete and tangible into the arena of movement, cause and effect. The further one moves away from the everyday and concrete to the rare and intangible, the more questionable shorthand descriptions become.

In the area of the human spirit where cojectivity is experienced as supremely real yet beyond our grasp, the use of language and names runs into real problems. We have all had arguments about such things as colour. ('She was wearing a wonderful dress; it was an exquisite blue.' 'Blue! It was never blue, it was definitely green.' And so on.)

The area where colours merge into one another is a matter of subjective experience and perception, and different people choose to call the same reality by different names. Yet the reality itself doesn't alter. No matter what people choose to call a colour, it is what it is by the nature of its reflective properties. Take a cojective approach and external realities concerned with the visible, touchable, smellable, tastable or audible, disappear. Although something may not be detectable by our five senses it is still real, sometimes seemingly more so, than the concrete and tangible. And it is that, as I've already noted, that gives meaning to life, a reality beyond mere material existence.

It isn't surprising, therefore, that humanity has given lots of names to the cojective experience, known technically as 'nominalisations' because they have no actual content. 'God' is the greatest nominalisation of all – there's nothing concrete beyond the word itself. Politicians love such terms for that very reason. When they promise to *modernise* something or *reform* something, listen out for what *exactly* they intend to do. Concrete actions are seldom spoken of. Nominalisations make real communication difficult because the listener has to attach meaning to a vague proposition. Of course, within particular groups of people the name they have chosen binds them in their own understanding (I use the word 'bind' advisedly). Yet it has been my experience that, once you scratch the surface of any group understanding of the cojective, you will find differing interpretations underneath. And, of course, the more clearly a group defines its experience using the limited form of linguistics, the more it will be alienated from another group who also wish to define the experience clearly, but using different names and words.

In a town I know quite well there are two churches within a long stone's throw of each other. Both are Church of England, yet it would be true to say that they express their understanding of religion very differently, using very different words. One is High Church Catholic, the other Evangelical. If pushed, at an intellectual level they will agree that the god they worship (the lower case 'g' is intentional for reasons we'll soon appreciate) is the same one, but that is as far as it goes. It is clear to both groups of people that 'the others' are using words and symbols that are really not a true representation of their god at all. This division between believers of the same faith can be multiplied millions of times over among different faiths, beliefs and viewpoints. And let us not run away with the idea that only the religious define the cojective experience so narrowly. Those who take very different stances can be equally dogmatic in their definitions.

In the 1940s and 1950s some of those who followed the Behaviourist school of psychology insisted that cojectivity and cognition (inner experience and thought) were either non-existent or simply the result of conditioning and reinforcement. By labelling their cojective experience people tend to limit and confine it. In this way cojectivity is projected as an exterior objective reality to be believed in by other people. Philosophy, religion, science or art can all conspire to make their own particular reality a universal reality, and the name they give this reality becomes the focus for creeds, doctrines, dogmas and institutions.

In putting a name to anything, even something as mundane and simple as a teacup, what we're doing is projecting outwards from our own complex understanding – which has taken us a lifetime to build up – a single word or perhaps a phrase, the meaning of which we expect the listener to grasp in its entirety. When you're being told about something or someone, you create a picture in your mind from the words the other person is using – you are creating a reality out of words. Of course, in the absence of the actual person or object, the reality you're creating is *yours* not theirs. When you eventually meet the described person in the flesh, or see the object for itself, your reaction is probably 'It is nothing like I thought it would be'. If it is a person you encounter, you may be too polite to say so.

This common experience of being 'misled' by others' descriptions is true of the tangible, solid matter of our everyday existence. How much more so must it be when we're trying to communicate in the realm of the cojective? In all matters of the 'heart' or 'spirit', areas where empirical objective proof is not possible, names and descriptions must always be regarded as provisional and never completely adequate.

Each of us has our own unique history, our own perceptions constructed over many years, and our own psychological type. So it is only to be expected that our cojective experiences will be described in differing ways, and be given different names. Trouble occurs when any individual or group insists that their particular description or name is definitively correct. When I was a small boy I thought all foreigners were stupid. At least we (the English) used the right words to talk, while they all used gobbledegook! Fortunately, I'm not quite so jingoistic these days. I have never mastered a second language, but I'm increasingly aware of the problems involved in simply trying to use the one that I do have, using it to build bridges that will unite, rather than create walls of division and isolation.

On a poster that I bought a few years ago, there was a picture of rather puzzled looking apes. The caption read: '**I know you believe**

**you understand what you think I said, but I'm not sure you realise, what you heard is not what I meant.'**

When we do not understand what another person is saying to us, or when we fail to make ourselves understood, we place one more brick in the wall that divides us one from another. Words are so important to the human race. By uttering a few words, millions of pounds may be lost or gained, wars started or stopped, relationships ended or begun. Both the written and spoken word have enormous potential for good and evil. Yet we tend to be so careless with them. So often we give insufficient thought to whether or not what we're saying is understood. And equally, how often do we stop to check whether we have heard the other person accurately?

When speaking with a colleague recently who was very anti-religion, we discovered that we do, in fact, have very similar beliefs – that is, we agreed on what was fundamentally important in life. Language and words had been a barrier because we had failed to delve below the surface meaning (a meaning different for both of us). We had created walls by simply not taking the time really to understand what the other was saying. The bridge we have subsequently built, a bridge that has benefited both of us, is constructed of the same words, but this time we've given ourselves the time really to listen to each other.

The cojective approach to life, on the other hand, assumes that what we have in common – our humanity – is a greater power than that which divides us. Whatever other occupation a cojective person may pursue, bridge building will always be a prime objective, and the tools we have most commonly at our disposal are words.

# CHAPTER 4

## Who are you?

The title for this chapter comes from Lewis Carroll's *Alice's Adventures in Wonderland*:

> 'Who are you?' said the Caterpillar. This was not an encouraging opening for a conversation. Alice replied, rather shyly. 'I – I hardly know sir, just at the present – at least I know who I was when I got up this morning, but I think I must have been changed several times since then.' 'What do you mean by that?' said the Caterpillar sternly. 'Explain yourself!' 'I can't explain myself, I'm afraid sir', said Alice, 'because I'm not myself, you see.'

At parties and other gatherings, when we meet somebody new the usual first question is 'What do you do?' not 'Who are you?' It's so much easier to define ourselves, and others, in terms of occupation, than to say how we see ourselves as people. Again, jobs help us to pigeonhole one another; a sort of shorthand. I have often wondered what it would be like to be a sex-therapist at a party – probably a real conversation stopper. (Although I guess it would depend on the party!)

Yet what we *do* surely matters less than who we are. Our personal histories, genes, physique and psychology all combine to make some occupations more likely than others, of course. For instance, I don't believe I'm psychologically equipped to harbour Mr Universe ambitions, which is just as well. My 5ft 8in stature, slight stoop and none too thin waistline, would make it a pretty unrealistic hope. And so it is for many people – circumstances and perception conspire against them finding a career path that's compatible with who they really are. Many are trapped in an occupation or lifestyle that feels repressive, and denies them the opportunity to express their true selves. And by 'repressive' I don't necessarily mean work that's simply repetitive or uninteresting, but rather a job in which the individual finds they're not free to be themselves. A high-flying lawyer, doctor or businessman or woman, on an income that most would envy, can feel less than fulfilled and repressed because they aren't being true to themselves. The course of our lives is very often dictated by our social position, our parents' ambitions for us and the education that has been available to us. Once set on a course, especially a career calling for long and expensive training, changing direction can be difficult. Or if we're in a job calling for little or no skill, and our education and training have not been all they could be, it's difficult to imagine how things might be different.

In Western society, where our very identity as well as what we do is an expression of our social status, it is often difficult for people to know who they really are. Like Alice they're confused. Part of the spirit of our age is a feeling so many people have of disconnectedness. It has been described as a 'spiritual vacuum' and has prompted many to call for a 'return to religion' or reassertion of 'moral values'. Yet I believe these calls are misguided. Both religious beliefs and moral values are concrete and objective expressions of a cojective understanding. They will resonate with some, but miss the point with a great many more. Those who make such a call for a return to religion, or the establishment of a particular set of moral values, are simply wanting to make universal a set of beliefs or values that happens to suit them. All too often these systems or values do nothing to help the individual to live life more fully and more 'humanly', or be able to answer the question, 'Who are you?' Far from it, such systems and values act as yet another set of external and objective criteria to which the unfortunate individual must conform.

None of which is to say I'm anti-religion or ready to dismiss moral values. But I am against both when, instead of offering guidelines, possibilities and signposts, they, or more accurately the way they're used, become inflexible systems posing as the 'truth' for every individual. When that happens, religion and morality become instruments of oppression and conformity, equivalent to anything that the pressures of an industrialised society or secular state can impose.

The real spiritual malaise that so many 21st century people are experiencing – a feeling of disconnectedness and of nothing having any real meaning – emerges not from a decline in religion and morality, but from people feeling alienated from themselves. **'I can't explain myself,' said Alice, 'because I'm not myself, you see.'**

Being separated from who we really are is, at worst, a death-dealing experience. It saps our energy and, for many people, leads to sickness and ill-health, both mental or psychological and physical. For several decades, in the West especially, material affluence and security have been expected to supply the answer, to somehow fill our existential emptiness and give life its proper meaning. Like most other things, material prosperity is, in itself, neither good nor bad – we can make of it what we will. But to expect it to fill our personal spiritual vacuum is likely to lead to more discomfort in the end, rather than less.

Several years ago a colleague of mine related a conversation he'd had with one of Britain's leading industrialists who said to my friend, 'Well, I've reached the top, I've got everything money can offer, but what the hell is it all about?'

To pursue a goal and then find there is nothing worthwhile at the end of the search is a devastating experience, especially if it has taken you most of your life to get there. The quest for the spirit is a quest for meaning, for fulfilment, both for yourself and those around you. To be a truly spiritual person is not to be religious, or pious or even 'nice' (how cloying that word is). It is to be truly yourself, to be integrated, whole and at-one.

The spiritual journey is not something alien to humankind. Nor is it some religious peculiarity entailing suspension of rational thought and the wholesale acceptance of some creedal system. Rather, it is that which enables every woman, man, boy and girl, to discover and be what they most fully and naturally are. It is as natural to our human state as eating, breathing or sex, but because the word 'spirituality' has been appropriated almost exclusively by religion, it is thought by many to have nothing to do with them. If you are one of those who attach the word 'spirit' or 'spiritual' exclusively to particular religious ideas, this next sentence is for you:

The world of the spirit, spirituality and the spiritual journey are defined in this book as human activities, the essence of our common human experience, and the means of self-fulfilment.

Religion may be one wholly valid expression of this fundamental human activity, of course, but it certainly isn't your only choice. And, like anything else, it can act as a distraction from the journey as much as a support. But more of that later.

In our society, seeking to know oneself is often considered to be almost unhealthy. Those who try counselling or therapy simply to gain greater insight into themselves are sometimes thought of as self-indulgent, selfish or just a little odd. Yet what could be more important than really to know yourself? If we do not, our lives are likely to remain unfulfilled, our relationships with others never truly profound or genuine, our motivation for doing almost anything probably seen as suspect, and those with whom we live and work will certainly feel the pain of our own fragmented being. Denied self-knowledge we're inevitably limited, and to some degree at least, dysfunctional. What we do not know about we have no opportunity to develop, change or control. Yet it's possible that acquiring self-knowledge can become just another toy to possess or game to play. Like all forms of learning, it's the way it is used – positively, negatively or not at all – that matters and which is up to the individual. The simple acquisition of self-knowledge alone is no guarantee that it will be used for the good, either of ourselves or others.

But without self-knowledge we're forever at the mercy of our own neurotic needs, the opinions of others, the latest fashion, the need to succeed (measured by standards other than our own), our physical looks or youthful appearance... and so on.

Want of self-knowledge takes us on a never-ending search for meaning and worth – all of it imbibed from the clamorous offerings of our surrounding culture. Our value, by this measure, is found not in who we are, for that is unknown territory, but in conforming to an objective standard set by others. And the source of that standard? Other people projecting their own quest for identity and meaning. This circular chasing of illusions is caught in the hollow looks and false smiles at many social gatherings the world over. With some people it is so blatant that it almost becomes an art form in itself: state-of-the-art shallowness.

I am, of course, talking about people fortunate enough to enjoy a sufficiency (and then some) of life's physical needs. Those who struggle day-to-day merely to survive have hollow looks for quite different reasons, mostly despair and hunger. Their smiles, when they come, are well-earned and genuine, and meaning is found in simple basics, a crust of bread or a bowl of rice. The poor know the real meaning of life. It is in countries insulated by affluence that many people, in the race to be somebody in a material sense, lose sight of their true selves. This is no new insight: Hindu religion and Buddhist philosophy call it Maya (illusion), while Jesus put it quite simply: **'What does it profit a man if he gains the whole world and loses or forfeits himself?' (Luke 9:25).**

Notice Jesus says 'loses himself'. Knowledge of our self is essential for psychological wholeness; it is enshrined in all the great religions and philosophies of the world, but does not belong to them. This fundamental truth – that human beings need to know themselves and then *be* themselves, in order to live a substantially fulfilled life in relationship with others – can, is and will be expressed in many different ways. You may not trust religion, psycho-talk may give you the heeby-jeebies, and philosophy may leave you cold – no matter. It's there in all the best legends, myths, stories, novels and movies. Knowing yourself is about embracing both the good and the dark side of your nature; wholeness comes not from denying our 'dragons and monsters', but from facing up to them. (Look what happened to Sleeping Beauty when the bad fairy wasn't invited to the party. More about this in the next chapter.)

The spiritual quest (the quest for the Holy Grail), is the quest to find ourselves, to be ourselves, and to live our lives as fully functioning human beings. Whatever there may or may not be beyond this life, and objectively we cannot know what it is, right now we are human beings. There can be no higher calling than to live our lives in a fully human way. If we wish to dress it up in religious language, fine, but the spiritual journey is for all of humanity, secular and religious alike. The reality will be the same – we simply call it by different names.

# CHAPTER 5

## Becoming who I am

In his marvellous little book *Why am I afraid to tell you who I am?* John Powell answers this question in a nutshell. It is taken from a conversation with a friend: **'I am afraid to tell you who I am, because, if I tell you who I am, you may not like who I am, and it's all that I have.'**

Fear of rejection makes us put up barriers, for probably the most painful psychological experience known to humanity is the isolation we feel if we're abandoned or rejected. We learn at a very early age that it is better to conform to someone else's standards and patterns, to be accepted on their terms, than to meet with disapproval for being ourselves. From the word go, our lives are moulded by our parents and other care-givers who simply impose on us the same standards and expectations that were applied to them. It is largely an un-thought-out process that repeats the patterns that are familiar and therefore safe. 'Safe' in this context doesn't mean that life within the family is good and wholesome; often nothing could be further from the truth. 'Safe' means not having to change anything, not having to think, not having to ask awkward questions about our own upbringing, our standards, assumptions and prejudices.

'Safety' is maintaining the status quo whatever the cost. And the cost is high – it can be denial of our true self. In this way the saying from the Hebrew Scriptures makes perfect psychological sense. While in its original context it was God who punished the guilty by **'visiting the iniquity of the parents upon the children and the children's children, to the third and fourth generations'** (Exodus 34:7), we now realise that it doesn't take a vengeful deity to do this. Human beings maintain patterns of behaviour from one generation to the next, probably well beyond the third and fourth generation.

To alter the pattern or break the mould, to question the values and norms of our family and society is a tremendously dangerous business. We run the risk of becoming outcast, of finding ourselves alone in a hostile world. And so we conform. We continue the habits and patterns, thoughts and behaviours that confirm us in our role. But so often that role isn't really us at all. We spend our lives fighting against the grain of who we really are in order not to feel bad about being rejected by a system into which we don't really fit. It's a double bind – follow the herd and be less than oneself, or follow one's own path and risk rejection and loneliness. Because of our life-long conditioning the second choice is seldom grasped, we just stay with the herd, repeating with our children all the mistakes that were inflicted upon us. Fear keeps us safe, and safety prevents us from becoming who we really are. I am not casting blame here. It's no use blaming our parents, schoolteachers or any other care-giver for the way we are now, it is simply one of those laws (or lores) of life, that what goes around, comes around. And who has expressed it more pithily than Philip Larkin in his poem *This be the Verse*?

> *They fuck you up, your mum and dad.*
> *They may not mean to, but they do.*
> *They fill you with the faults they had*
> *And add some extra, just for you.*
>
> *But they were fucked up in their turn*
> *By fools in old-style hats and coats,*
> *Who half the time were soppy-stern*
> *And half at one another's throats.*
>
> *Man hands on misery to man.*
> *It deepens like a coastal shelf.*
> *Get out as early as you can,*
> *And don't have any kids yourself.*

Nor do I wish to imply that everything learned at our parent's knee is intrinsically bad. Living in a complex society requires both knowledge and rules for survival. 'Don't cross the road without looking both ways' is a rule worth holding onto if we wish to live long enough to ask questions about rules in the first place! Nor necessarily are the things we wish to reject bad in themselves, they may simply not be right for us, or relevant to our present situation. A simple and harmless illustration of this can be taken from my own home background.

On Sundays at dinner time (1.00pm sharp), we always had a roast joint of some description, followed almost invariably by a fruit pie – apple, rhubarb, plum, gooseberry etc with custard. It didn't occur to any of us that Sunday dinners could be any different. It took the introduction of my brother-in-law into the family to question our Sunday ritual. I think it was probably a hot summer's day, when a light snack or salad would have been more appropriate than a large roast, when he queried the reason for it. I can remember my mother's answer quite distinctly all these years later, 'Cos that's what my mum always cooked at home.' While we all enjoyed my mother's cooking, and in itself there was nothing at all wrong with the traditional fare, on occasions when more appropriate food might have been served, it wasn't even considered because we were all enslaved by Granny's Sunday routine.

Of course in Granny's day, having a roast on Sunday had practical implications. It meant that there was always cold meat in the house for Monday, which was wash day. With no labour saving devices, and a large family (eight children), wash day was an all-day activity. From the lighting of the fire under the copper first thing in the morning, to hanging out the last load late in the afternoon, there was little time to stop and prepare food. Sunday's cold meat came into its own. So what for one generation was a practical solution to a particular problem, became for the next generation a family 'rule' that was never questioned. This harmless example (none of us was scarred by eating roasts and fruit pies) shows how easily we become entrapped by rituals lifted unthinkingly from the past.

Of course, there are those who, for whatever reason, decide to break the mould. Perhaps because their parents managed it to a lesser degree and so gave them permission to be real. Perhaps it was because the pain of being unreal simply became too great, the cost too high, so the risk of exposure became a price worth paying. Maybe it came about as a result of a breakdown, mental, psychological or physical, or in a relationship – the end of a marriage or partnership. Or perhaps it was that the partner we chose to live with gave us sufficient love, space and security to begin to let go of the past.

There are many reasons people feel freed to undertake the voyage of discovery towards their true selves, leaving behind the security of the familiar and venturing into the unknown. But, whatever the main motivation, two factors are almost certainly in play. First, there will be, at the least, poor understanding by their family and friends, and perhaps outright hostility. All the norms of their life are seen as being challenged by this action, and, as I have already said, keeping the status quo has a lot of energy invested in it. Second, the reason will involve 'fighting with dragons'. In all great tales and myths, the hero has to go on a journey, he (for usually it is a he, but despite the sexist language, it is symbolic of the whole of humanity), encounters many trials and battles, overcoming beasts of every kind, eventually to arrive at his destination – to find the treasure or rescue the princess. The fighting with 'beasts and dragons' is symbolic of our own encounter with the darker side of our own personality. It is something we would all rather ignore, pretend isn't there, or hope will go away. Yet this encounter is vital to our spiritual journey; without it we can never become truly ourselves, and will always see and hate in others those aspects of our own personalities we have been unable to come to terms with.

In the story of the Sleeping Beauty the wicked fairy was not invited to the celebrations of the Princess's birth. What might have happened had she been included? Well, for sure there would have been an air of uncertainty, people would have felt uncomfortable, and recognition would have had to be given to the power of darkness within their midst. To avoid such feelings of discomfort, she was excluded from the gathering. Yet despite the universal discomfort, inviting the wicked fairy would probably have mitigated the dreadful consequences that followed. Failing to recognise and include our own 'dark side' has the same destructive results.

The greatest example of this in our recent history was the persecution of the Jewish people (and other minority groups) by the Nazi regime. In the 1930s the German economy was facing disaster. However, rather than take collective responsibility for their problems, the Nazi element in society projected their own inadequacies and frustrations onto another group, the Jews. So great was the evil done at that time that the Holocaust reverberates even today. And the damage done to the collective psyche of the Jewish people also plays out today. Tragically, the collective guilt of Western nations, and the fear and pain of many of the survivors and their relatives, resulted in patterns being repeated yet again. Oppression of one people by another for the perceived greater good of the oppressor will simply feed into cycles of violence ad infinitum. The current oppression of the Palestinians by the Israeli state, and the conditions in which the Palestinian people are forced to live, will inevitably produce a violent reaction.

And so the wheel keeps turning. Jihad *is* the answer, but it must be Jihad that tackles the individual's and the nation's own *inner* journey, not Jihad that directs violence towards others. This is the greater Jihad, the struggle to root out everything that is sinful and rebellious in our own hearts and minds. True Jihad for all people, of all faiths and none, is the journey inwards, and is there to recognise the oneness of all humanity.

What plays out on the world stage through mass violence and conflict is, in miniature, what we're all capable of at an individual level. To a greater or lesser degree, when we fail to recognise our own culpability in the 'wrongs' of our personal lives and the life of society, we project the fault onto others. Perhaps it will be known individuals or groups, or more than likely the proverbial 'they'. 'They' should have done something. 'They' always get it wrong. 'They' really means anybody but me.

Part of the spiritual quest must be to discover and confront those parts of ourselves we would rather deny: to take responsibility for our actions and to accept that whatever the past held for us, the present moment is our responsibility. We can make of it what we will, but if we choose negative actions with equally negative consequences, we must not try to lay the blame at anybody else's door.

Apart from psychotic personalities (those who, mentally or psychologically, are not in touch with reality), who are few in number, there is among people generally an almost universal understanding of what is right and what is wrong. Customs may vary from culture to culture, but they do not usually affect the basic norms of a society. The fundamental behaviours that enable people to live together are enshrined in all the great religions and philosophies, both past and present: to commit no murder, not to steal, to honour a marriage relationship (however that is defined), to respect the rights of another, to act with mercy and justice...

Each culture and time in history may express it differently, but at a cojective level, people always know what is right. The spiritual journey is concerned with recognising those areas of ourselves that are not fully in accord with all that is good, and taking responsibility for them. It is equally concerned with finding ways in which individuals can be truest to themselves, while also seeking the highest good for others in society. The spiritual journey cannot be taken alone. The very nature of the human spirit is that it is experienced most fully cojectively, and not in isolation. People who focus on themselves, either their own personal salvation and piety, or their wealth, power and personal status, are being sidetracked from the reality of the spiritual life.

The spiritual journey must therefore be to discover who I am as an individual, to be true to that self regardless of the conditioning of the past or the pressures of the present, and to live my life as fully as I can. But always, always, this is mediated through interaction with others – at home, in the office, at school, in the factory, on the farm or in the monastery – and with the best interests of others at heart. Spirituality is a here-and-now thing, a fully human thing. It is what brings out the best in people and makes for creative and happy lives.

But it doesn't just happen. Like any art – and learning to live our lives fully is an art – it requires practice and discipline. Nobody becomes a proficient painter or concert pianist by simply wishing it. Much time and effort, and usually more than a little heartache, must be devoted to it. So if you wish to live your life just as fully, it will call for just as much dedication as the mastery of any art, sport or other discipline. The difference is that the spiritual journey is a life-long one. So great is our potential that we will never fully achieve it in the average 70 or 80 years that we live.

Most of us have encountered people who have spent their lives on a spiritual journey (whether or not it has any religious content). They tend to be open, flexible, full of love and compassion, interesting, interested and a joy to be with. We have also encountered those who have taken the opposite path (again, regardless of whether it has any religious content). They tend to be narrow, bigoted, self-centred, mean, boring and a real pain to spend time with.

Within us all there is the potential to become either fully human and fully alive – a joy to ourselves and those around us – or to become mean, self-centred and only half receptive to the joy of living. The choice and the responsibility are ours. It's a journey that's never too late to start, but beware, leave it too long and your perception will tell you that it's just too difficult, not worth the effort, or that it doesn't exist at all. The longer you have spent defending the status quo, in trying to locate your personal value outside yourself, then the harder it will be to change direction. As Gerald W Johnson so aptly puts it: 'The closed mind, if closed long enough, can be opened by nothing short of dynamite.'

Those readers who remember *The Last Battle* by C S Lewis will recall that toward the end, a group of dwarfs are convinced that they are captive in a dark and smelly stable. In fact, they are free in the fresh air and daylight.

> 'Are you blind?' said Trinian. 'Ain't we all blind in the dark?' said Diggle. 'But it isn't dark, you stupid Dwarfs,' said Lucy. 'Can't you see? Look up! Look round! Can't you see the sky and the trees and the flowers? Can't you see me?' 'How in the name of Humbug can I see what ain't there…'

No matter what evidence was placed before them, the Dwarfs could see only what they believed to be the case. Like the Dwarfs, many people have invested too much in their narrow visions and defence of the status quo, even to begin to conceive of a different reality.

Many modern films and stories reflect the ancient myths and legends. And no wonder, for they are our story, our hopes and our fears. At the end of Steven Spielberg's film *Hook*, the adult Peter Pan, having been utterly challenged and changed by his return to Never Land, discovers something more of his true self. The film ends with him saying: 'To live will be an awfully big adventure.' Such is the spiritual journey, the journey of 'becoming who I am' – but it's for real.

# CHAPTER 6

## Never on a Friday

Some years ago, on Good Friday, two of my wife's cousins came to visit. We talked for a couple of hours over tea and hot-cross buns, and when they were preparing to go, the question of supper arose. They said they'd been out to buy fish to mark Good Friday, and when we said we were having pork chops, a look of disbelief crossed their faces. Neither of them was particularly religious, yet they believed it was somehow fitting not to eat meat on Good Friday. While Ruth and I, both ordained members of the Church were having meat, our non-religious cousins were holding to a ritual retrieved from the past.

The encounter took me back more than 40 years to my local pub. Part of an overheard conversation struck me quite forcefully at the time, and has stayed with me ever since. It was one of those conversations that crop up from time to time about going to church and being religious. I can hear the part that struck home even now; it was uttered by a middle-aged cockney woman: 'Naw, I'm very religious, you'll never catch me with meat in the 'ouse on a Friday.'

Despite my youth at the time and poor understanding, I felt in my bones that this statement was an important one. It managed to sum up all the misconceptions about religion in one short sentence. It's what happens when something cojective gets turned into something objective. Religion is a past master at doing this. It so often manages to turn the great adventure of living into a set of rules that deny an individual the freedom of self-discovery. Rather than becoming a vehicle helping people to become fully themselves, to live their lives creatively as fully functioning human beings, religion becomes a strait-jacket that limits and controls. What should free people to become who they really are, more often than not, to use the (somewhat sexist) words of W H Auden, turns them into *tight-assed old maids of both sexes*. How has this happened? How have the liberating teachings of some great human beings been turned into narrow dogma that constricts and divides humanity?

One of the reasons I felt compelled to write this book was the response I received to a short piece I'd written for a parish magazine: 'Religion is bad for you'. It obviously struck a chord with a lot of people. I got phone calls from many who had given up the struggle with organised religion but still identified with a spiritual life. While still practising their faith, they felt ill at ease with it and welcomed the 'breath of fresh air' the article represented.

Whenever I speak of spirituality rather than religion, I find people sigh with relief that somebody is actually expressing what they feel in their innermost being. It also has to be said that some were offended by the article, and found it sufficient reason to cancel their place on the parish retreat I was conducting that year. But I'm not primarily writing for those who are content with their religion, but those who struggle with it, or simply reject it.

The following passage is the bulk of that same article:

> Religion is certainly bad for you. At best it helps to contain neurosis. At worst it causes the neurosis and narrow-mindedness which lead to behaviour patterns that are unhealthy and damaging, both to the individual concerned, and to those with whom they come into contact.
>
> I believe this to be true, yet I remain a Priest; why? I remain a priest because I am convinced that the fundamental principle which underlies all the great religions is true. Yet the principle itself cannot be 'captured' within the religion. There is a supreme paradox here, for as soon as the subject of religion is transmitted in anything other than its original form – that is experience – it ceases to be what it actually is. Subject becomes object. Religion has the effect of transforming the reality of experience into a codified

system which represents experience, but which is always at least one step removed from it. Religion is healthy only when it is understood as a secondhand representation of an existential reality. Let me give you an example.

You go on holiday to one of the Greek Islands. In your room there is a wonderful photograph of the sunset across the bay – in fact the view from the front of your hotel. Every night you sit in your room looking at the photograph, but never see the real thing. When you return, you tell your friends, 'they have the most wonderful sunsets, I can't wait to go and see them again.'

Religious belief, like the photograph, is secondhand. It points to a reality beyond itself, a reality which will be experienced differently by every individual. Every religion, and every denomination or sect within every religion has its own 'photograph'. Each proclaims 'this is the truth, believe in this'. Religion turns subjective experience into objective reality, it bids us abandon real living in exchange for a safe and sterile belief. Believing there is a sunset by enjoying a photo is hardly a substitute for the real thing. I remain a priest because I am committed to the path, not of religion, but of spirituality. Spirituality is not about believing set things, reciting certain creeds, or behaving in predictable ways. Spirituality is concerned with every individual finding their own truth, seeing their own sunset and experiencing their own God. Religion can play a part in this, but only a part, and one needs to cleve to it very lightly.

As soon as it becomes important in itself we are drawn into idolatry, into secondhand living. Jesus said to the religious leaders of his day that tax gatherers and prostitutes would enter the Kingdom before them. Why? Because in their non-religious way they were seeking the truth, while the religious people thought that they had already found it! Religion is bad for you therefore, not in itself- few things are bad in themselves – but when we fail to recognise it for what it is. When we give ourselves to religion as if it is the truth, instead of a (frequently very poor) representation, we remain dead to the truth and dead to ourselves – for who continues to journey when he thinks he's already arrived? Use religion then as one of your many aids on the spiritual journey, but do not become too attached to it, for if you do, it will surely be the death of your spiritual life.


I naturally speak from the perspective and perceptions of a priest in the Christian tradition. Yet any tradition can become prey to ritual for its own sake, or give it a significance it should not have. Some years ago I occasionally shared in a meditation group led by a Buddhist monk. At the end of the evening he would be given a cup of tea, but it could not be handed to him directly by the woman who was hosting the evening. A minor ritual involved ensuring that no direct contact took place between the monk and the woman. There seemed to me to be something incongruous about this. Buddhism is very hot on detachment, yet there seemed to be a lot of palaver involved in simply receiving a cup of tea. In ensuring total detachment from women, there seemed to be an unnecessary attachment to ritual. It reminded me of the following traditional story.

> Two strict Christian monks, on their way back to their monastery, found an exceedingly beautiful woman at the river bank. Like them, she wanted to cross to the other side, but the water was high and fast flowing. The woman was on her way to a wedding, so was dressed in her finest clothes. Seeing her predicament, one of the monks lifted her onto his shoulders and carried her across. His brother monk was horrified. For a long time he berated his brother on his disregard for the Rule. Had he forgotten he was a monk and was not supposed to touch a woman? What was he thinking of? And worse, actually carrying her on his back! What would people think? What would the Abbot think? What would the Pope say if he ever heard of it? The offending monk listened to the endless denunciations with calmness and patience. Finally, he interrupted: 'Brother, I put the woman down at the riverbank. Why are you still carrying her?'

I am not against ritual; it can add a dimension to life that is very worthwhile. Yet it must never become important in itself. When ritual becomes more important than people, or when it becomes death-dealing rather than life-enhancing, then it is time to ask just what we are doing, and why we're doing it. Sometimes religious rituals continue long after they have any justification or significance.

Some years ago Ruth and I attended worship at a very high Anglican church. There came the point in the service when the priest was censing the altar (waving a container of burning incense [the thurible] at a given object or person.) He was wearing a sleeveless garment (chasuble), and as he went round the altar, the deacon and sub-deacon were trotting round after him hanging onto his shoulders as though attached with superglue. Ruth looked incredulous. 'What on earth are they doing?' she hissed in my ear. This ridiculous ritual was a hangover from a time when the priest wore a very heavy, sleeved chasuble. The deacon and sub-deacon would accompany the priest, holding up the garment so that his arms were free to swing the thurible. What was once a sensible necessity, had turned into an empty and absurd convention. It reminded me of another wonderful story, this time from Hindu tradition:

> When the guru sat down to meditate each evening, his cat, which roamed freely around the ashram, would often get in the way and disturb those who were also meditating. So he decided to tie up the cat at meditation time. After a while the guru died, but his followers continued to tie up the cat when they were meditating. When eventually the cat died too, the guru's disciples bought another cat so that it could also be tied up. Many years later, academic treatises were written by the guru's scholarly disciples on the importance of tying up a cat during their practice of meditation.

As I write this chapter I am aware of very many examples where ritual has become divorced from original meaning.

To do something 'religiously' has come to mean according to a fixed routine, or with unswerving loyalty to a habit. Far from enabling people to explore their cojective experiences together, religion has replaced exploration with belief in certain objective criteria. Scripture, creeds, doctrines and dogmas have become ends in themselves, actually preventing and proscribing the possibility of growth and development in those who rigidly adhere to them.

Over the years we have seen horrendous outcomes when religion is taken to extreme. In 1978, 914 people died in the mass suicide in Jonestown, Guyana. April 1993 saw the horrific consequences of the Branch Davidian Sect tragedy in Waco, Texas, that led to the deaths of men, women and children under the influence of the psychopathic 'messiah' David Koresh. And in 1994 48 people died under the influence of the sect known as the Order of the Solar Temple. All took literally the apocalyptic books of the Bible (allegories that should be regarded more like fiction than prophesy) which led to a doomsday scenario. And a doomsday scenario was exactly what was planned in Japan by the Aum Shrinri Kyo cult when they released a lethal nerve gas into the Tokyo subway in March 1995. And since the turn of this century, we have seen mass destruction and the deaths of thousands inspired by religious fundamentalism so often fuelled by a sense of injustice and intolerance. Indeed, religious fervour is often the root cause of violent extremism.

Those extreme cases demonstrate what can happen when religious fervour overrides the need for the individual to discover and explore his or her own path. It is an example of the need for security and certainty sustained by a literalist interpretation of the Bible, or other religious text, being exploited to the $N^{th}$ degree. Yet these excesses are but an extreme form of what most religious dogma sets forth in more diluted form, whether it is the traditions and creeds of the Catholic Church, the reliance on scripture of the Evangelical Church, the experience of the 'holy spirit' in charismatic churches, the infallibility of the direct revelation of the Koran in Islam, or being the 'People of God' of the Jewish tradition...

Every religion in some way objectifies the truth in a set of writings and practices, and actively discourages its followers from looking beyond its own boundaries. The result of this is any number of religions and sects which all claim to have, if not the monopoly, certainly a clearer vision, of the truth than anybody else. In a world that always has been, and always will be, an uncertain and dangerous place, the certainty offered by religion can be a refuge for those who feel uncertain about themselves and uncertain about the world in which they live. Yet I believe religious certainty to be a contradiction in terms. As many atheists point out, there is no proof of God's existence. We 'know' of God experientially not empirically, and two people's experiences can differ totally from each other's. The old certainties of religion will no longer do (if they ever did), because they fail to stay true to the human spirit, which will not, and cannot, be confined by systems and patterns of belief. The cojective spirit within each person is diminished if it is hemmed in by a belief system, no matter what form it takes, and prevented from connecting with another human being.

People can be 'religious' about more than just religion. Science, politics, materialism and 'good works', can all take on the nature of religion when they become ends in themselves. The 'New Age Movement', which in many ways was a response to, and a rejection of, conventional religion, was as prone to the dangers of confining the truth as anything else. The 'alternative society', if it fails to take account of what it is an alternative to, will be as lop-sided as the society or belief system it has rejected. Each swing of the pendulum from one set of values to another inevitably continues to get the balance wrong, but from the opposite direction. The spiritual path is about finding balance, finding and using those things we value, while rejecting others. No single religion or belief system gets the balance right. We need to discriminate and find those elements that resonate with our own spirit, and enable us to live our lives to the full. To paraphrase a certain well-known Jewish rabbi: 'Religion is made for humanity, not humanity for religion' (See St Mark's Gospel 2:27).

Everyone who is religious by upbringing or inclination, needs to address the following question: how much of what you do or say during prescribed worship do you know the reason for? It's a question worth answering because it can lead to greater understanding of what you do and liberation from unnecessary clutter.

One last story to illustrate religious clutter. In one church I knew (as in many others) the choir always turned to face the altar when they said the creed. All new choir members were taught to do the same. When I asked, I found that nobody knew why they were doing it. What's more, when the nave altar was in use, when they turned they faced away from the altar actually being used. And to make a complete nonsense of the whole thing, the axis of the church was reversed, so that instead of facing east (the traditional reason for turning), they were facing west. As far as I know, they still follow this ritual. The guru's cat would have been proud of them.

In the second part of this book I'll be looking at ways in which we can practice religion without becoming religious. As I have already suggested, religion is certainly one way in which the spirit of humanity can legitimately express itself. It isn't religion that is bad, but an exclusive and dogmatic attitude that often accompanies it.

To those who enjoyed the stories of the two monks and the guru's cat, I recommend Anthony de Mello's book *Song of the Bird*. It is an anthology of traditional stories from all over the world.

# CHAPTER 7

## Goodbye to 'God'

While I was still in theological college, back in 1980, the Cambridge theologian and Anglican priest Don Cupitt wrote a book, *Taking Leave of God.* Needless to say, with a title like that, and written by a priest, it was pretty controversial. But what I found disturbing wasn't the content – which I thought stimulating – but the attitude of some of my fellow theological students. I heard one say, 'It's a terrible book, I'm not going to read it.' In short, the condemnation focused on what the title suggested, without considering what Cupitt meant by it. People of all religious traditions over generations have been unwilling to let go – or worse, fearful of letting go – of the images of God that their traditions have taught them over time. My contention, however, is that unless we're prepared to say 'goodbye' to the God we've been brought up with, we'll never become truly spiritual human beings.

There are three reasons why I believe the spiritual life demands this. First, if there is a God – and that remains an open question throughout this book – there is no way we can know, in an empirical or scientific sense, that she does exist. There is nothing objective about our knowledge of God; rather, people experience something cojectively which they then call God (or whatever name a given religion uses). Certainly there is much religious practice and liturgy, as well as many scriptures, doctrines, creeds and dogmas, yet they merely reflect humanity's wish to make concrete that which is at once deeply important but insubstantial.

The fact remains that there is nothing, no evidence whatsoever, that there is a God. If there were, two things would follow. One, there would be far greater uniformity of belief. The present diverse nature of religious belief points to the fact that there is nothing unarguably objective about God. Even given what we know about perspective and perception, there would certainly be more universal agreement about God's nature if God was objectively knowable. Two, if there were any universal and objective evidence, then apart from those who might not be considered quite sane, there would be no possibility of anyone declaring him or herself agnostic or atheistic. But the fact is, millions of people the world over find either agnosticism or atheism the only credible position to hold.

But in recommending that we say 'goodbye' to God, I am not declaring myself an atheist, because it seems to me that atheism is as dotty as unquestioning belief. We can no more prove that God does not exist, than we can prove that she does. To prove the existence of something may be difficult, but to prove a negative – God's non-existence – is impossible. In saying 'goodbye to God', I am simply arguing for the letting go of old stereotypes and ideas *about* God, regardless of whether they're positive or negative.

You may have found it amusing, irritating, affirming, or even shocking, that I've been referring to God as 'she'. Of course, it is silly, but no more so than referring to God as 'he'. Any gender-specific term highlights the limits of our imagination. Some may think that speaking of God and sex in the same breath is blasphemous, but if we insist on using gender terminology, then we cannot avoid the obvious sexual connotation. To use 'he' and 'father' is to claim that God is a male. Push the point further and we can even legitimately ask: 'Does God have a penis?' If the answer is yes, it is immediately followed by the question, 'What for?' If the answer is no, then we can ask, 'In what way do we mean that God is male?' It becomes clear when we ask simple questions about God's genitals (or lack of them), that we have made God in our own image. That is not to say we have 'invented' God. As I've already noted, we have no evidence one way or the other about God's actual existence. But what we have clearly done is to imagine God in human likeness.

In early and primitive religions, God (or Gods) often took a female form. The Goddess was seen as the great womb out of which all life originally emerged. As man's part in procreation became accepted, so the Goddesses acquired a consort whose status gradually grew. Over the period covered by the Old and New Testaments, it was thought that the male seed harboured all the potential for new life. Like the seed of a flower, the seed of man needed only a fertile place to grow. Women were reduced to the status of 'grow bags' who could be considered 'barren' if they could not produce children. And as the process of creation became an exclusively male attribute, it's no wonder that God became a male figure. Note, however, that in Hinduism, where both male and female genitals are symbolically represented as objects of worship, the Gods are both male and female.

Not only does the sex of God arise from our own cultural understanding, but so does everything else. God as lord, king, majesty, warrior, servant and priest – all are products of our human conditioning and experience, which we then project onto the 'person' of God. In the chapter 'What's in a name?' I referred to God with a small 'g'. That's because whatever the reality of God may or may not be, those who differ about it are not differing about the reality (or lack of it), but about their image of God.

Out of the cojective experience of each group, an image of God is constructed, which is then worshipped and served as if it were real. Now there is nothing wrong with that, as long as we realise that that is what we're doing. If there is a God, then it, she or he can never be objectively known, only cojectively. To turn our cojective experience into an objective reality is to produce an idol. Hindus, Muslims, Christians and Jews as well as adherents of many other faiths and sects, all claim that the nature of God has been revealed to them. Yet all are different. If one is right then all the rest are wrong, which seems unlikely, or perhaps all can claim a partial truth, or all are completely wrong. To approach religion cojectively, though, is to accept that each person's experience or each faith is then culturally and historically expressed in objective form. Whatever the truth of the original experience, its objective expression will always be secondhand, at least one step removed from the experience itself.

Cojectivity lets every person experience their own truth and express it in their own way. It never wants to convert because it knows that one set of secondhand experiences is no better than another. The cojective person seeks to look beyond the objective manifestation to the experienced reality that lies beyond it. We need to say 'goodbye' to God, not to the reality – whatever that may be – but to the limited and inadequate expressions common to every religion, which when objectified and worshipped as the truth become no more than idols and totems.

To say 'goodbye' to God is to allow God to be whatever God actually is, without limiting it to our own image of the reality. If we allow God to be God, then we also need to allow ourselves to be ourselves. This is the second reason for saying 'goodbye'. In a previous chapter I spoke about our need to both know and be ourselves. So often, certainly within the Christian tradition, I come across people who are inhibited by their religion, rather than set free by it. People who, in their everyday lives, hold down important and responsible jobs, but on Sundays are reduced to nervous wrecks if asked to read a lesson in church. What is that about?

Why do people feel less at ease in church than almost anywhere else? I am not talking here of regular church-goers. The unease of people who are not regular worshippers is evident before the service begins. At almost every baptism, wedding or funeral I have conducted, nervous groups of people stand around outside the church until the last minute before going in. Certainly some of the tension and reluctance will arise from the occasion itself, some of it can be blamed on a last cigarette, and some of it will arise from the sheer alienation most non-church people feel about the building and its services. But there is, I am sure, something deeper too: an unease about God. The image so often presented by the Church is of a God who accepts you if, and only if...

If you conform to certain standards. If you give a proportion of your income. If you worship in this way and not that. If, if, if... There is a sense of having to deny some part of who we really are before we can be acceptable. For many people it has uncomfortable undertones of their family, their school, their work... always needing to be something else, something better than I am. There are, perhaps, some who feel that they're OK, loved and accepted just as they are, unconditionally. But so far I have not met even one because we all carry baggage from the past.

Even if theirs are the best-intentioned parents, most people receive the message that to be OK they need to adapt their responses to the wishes of others, to be less or more than they really are. But some parents, teachers and others who influence us when we are young, are not well intentioned. They can be cruel and bigoted and have little regard for the well-being of those in their care. Whether we've been lucky or unlucky in our upbringing, the effect is likely to be the same, differing only in degree: we feel the need to conform to standards set by another in order to be acceptable – 'I'll love you if...' And God has been tarred with the same brush. That isn't surprising, of course, given what I've said about us creating God in our own image. So God becomes the ultimate expression of whatever it is we feel oppressed by, the ultimate exemplar against which we must measure ourselves, and in so doing deny part of who we truly are.

But if there is a God, then this surely is the one being with whom we can be totally honest. We don't need to put on our Sunday best, literally or metaphorically, because this being must know us completely anyway. What a waste of time and energy trying to pretend we're something we are not. No, if God is, then we can be ourselves with God. We can swear at God and to God, about God and with God. In the introduction to his book *God for Nothing*, Richard MacKenna tells the story of a bereaved woman who, in her anger and frustration shouts out 'Fuck God and fuck the Church'. Her 'goodbye to God' was couched in earthy language that reflected her true feelings in that moment of despair. If anything is prayer, that is. It is a woman crying out in extremis. In the urgency of her need and desolation she is being herself, being real, and that is the most important gift we can offer any other being, human or divine.

Being able to say 'goodbye' to God is an essential part of our spiritual life. It enables us to let go of images that will always be inadequate expressions of a cojective experience, and it allows us to be real and be honest with ourselves, rather than conform to yet another external value which may not be our own. Both the above reasons for saying 'goodbye' to God are personal and individual. They free us from conditioning that is both cultural and historical, as well as personal, and enable us to discover for ourselves the reality that underlies literally millions of different images and codes of practice.

But the third reason for saying 'goodbye' to God is perhaps the most important, and certainly the most universal. Being able to say 'goodbye' is a recognition by me, that my brother atheist or my sister

Muslim do not need converting to my way of thinking, to my image of God. Rather, I need to understand, to listen. It is a recognition that their cojective experience is being expressed in a different language, with different names and images, but that at its heart lies the same reality.

If any conversion needs to take place, it is in my heart and understanding, so that I can see beyond the limits imposed on me by my race, colour, class (or caste) or my religious or secular beliefs. Not only does the religious person need to say 'goodbye' to God to be released from the dead hand of conditioning, but so does the secular atheist. You may think this sounds strange, and that the atheist has already said it once and for all. But we all have our 'gods' or sacred cows, beliefs that we hold onto because we feel comfortable with them. In discussions with atheists I often find that they have very set views about God and religion which they hold onto with the same tenacity as the devout believer. They have erected an Aunt Sally that is easily knocked down, and which enables them to maintain their position without much thought or effort. The atheist and the fundamentalist will often hold not dissimilar views about God and religion, it is just that one rejects it vehemently and the other believes it vehemently. Saying 'goodbye' to God means being prepared to let go of our beliefs, religious or secular, in order to try to understand the fundamental sameness of the human spirit.

There is so much about the evolutionary biologist Richard Dawkins that I admire. He has opened up the world of science, and biology in particular, to many with little or no such expertise, and for that he should be thanked. His incursions into religion and theology, however, are lamentable. He takes a literalist approach to religion that matches the worst excesses of the fundamentalist believer, as if such extremists represent the 'truth' of religion, which he then proceeds to demolish. I am grateful that he has exposed some of the more ridiculous aspects of religious belief and practice, which may well help people to utter that all important 'goodbye', but when he tries to apply scientific criteria to largely cojective experience I'm afraid he goes off half-cocked. Dawkins seems to have missed the point that religious language consists primarily of symbolic formulations depicting deep psychological and humanist phenomena. He comes at the subject with inappropriate techniques, rather as if he were trying to weigh colour: 'There are more things in heaven and earth, Horatio, than are dreamt of in your philosophy.'

There will be those, I know, within the Christian tradition, and probably other traditions, who will complain that what I propose represents a watering-down of the faith; to admit to the truth that lies within every human heart is to weaken their religion to the point of destruction. But where lies the real strength? Is it in having to cling to limited beliefs for the sake of security? Or is it in being open enough to accept that the truth is more comprehensive than any one individual or group can possibly fully know? How many wars and conflicts, how many arguments and broken relationships have occurred, and still do occur, because people are unwilling to say 'goodbye' to whatever they have erected as the god in their lives? To say 'goodbye' to whatever limits and confines, be it religious or secular, is to open up human creativity rather than its destructiveness. It is to occupy the middle ground – cojective understanding – which unites rather than divides.

When I was a fresh new Franciscan brother, I was, perhaps, rather too holy and pious (probably a right pain in the butt). I shunned ripe language and thought swearing rather unchristian. After a few months at the largest friary in Dorset, I was moved to the house in Liverpool, run at the time by David, a Canon in the Church, and senior industrial chaplain. There was a box on the common-room wall complete with mini-doors and a spotlight, and I assumed it probably concealed an icon or other holy painting. No chance. To my huge surprise I soon discovered the treasure within was nothing more hallowed than a dart-board, and when David missed a vital double and exclaimed 'Oh shit', I confess I was shocked – here was a senior priest swearing at an absurd triviality. But we talked about it. Very gently, David suggested that if everyone in the world stopped swearing tomorrow, the world would not be a much better place. But if everybody loved one another just a fraction more, the world would be transformed. I owe a lot to that holy man, because he helped me free myself of a lot of sacred cows, and begin the process of seeing life cojectively rather than in the black-and-white, two-dimensional – subject and object – terms with which I'd burdened myself.

Whatever your beliefs, religious or secular, live lightly with them, and pass beyond them to the reality that unites us all. It's a risky business, but it will help you embrace more fully the spirit of humanity, and your life will change direction – I guarantee it.

Being able to dismiss God, in whatever language and terms make sense to you, marks the beginning of true spirituality; it connects us to what is most real within us, and transcends our own restricted vision. It is the start of something big.

# CHAPTER 8

## Is anybody there?

This chapter is for Betty. Betty was a good friend with more than a little in common with my one-time pin-up girl (even clergymen are allowed pin-ups). But this one wouldn't drop comfortably into a Pirelli calendar. Mine was that marvellous actress and definitive Miss Marple, Joan Hickson. Outwardly, Joan and Betty shared quite a lot: both were small physically, and both were elderly and grey haired. The crucial similarity, though, a quality they shared with Agatha Christie's redoubtable Miss Marple, was their sharp-as-bacon-slicer minds.

Betty, like many of her generation, was a loyal member of the Church, but loyalty didn't mean switching off intellectually as soon as she walked through the church door. Betty's searching mind wasn't satisfied with hand-me-down formulations from a bygone age. She both wanted to believe and did believe in God, but a paternalistic figure who reigns on-high cut no ice with her. At the beginning of the 21st century many people like Betty want to express their spirituality in a religious and theistic way, but aren't prepared to be intellectually dishonest with themselves to do so. They (and I include myself in their number) want to find a formulation or understanding that doesn't depend on a first-century or medieval picture of God. And, as I have already pointed out, a picture or concept is all we can have.

If God does exist then, by definition, he, she or it will be beyond our comprehension and the best that we can do is create a 'picture' that most closely represents our experience, fractional and marginal though it may be. To my fellow theists (believers in a God of some sort) and especially to other Christians, it may seem shocking to propose that the God we 'create' accords with our own experiences and perceptions. But as I pointed out in the first chapter, this creative process is something we do all the time, even with limited and material objects.

I'm reminded of a story I heard on the radio told by Rabbi Lionel Blue.

> A man is standing at the edge of a vast cliff; as he looks over, there is nothing separating him from the rocks 500 feet below. Suddenly a gust of wind blows him over the edge. As he falls he grabs hold of a solitary small tree growing out of the cliff face. Below is certain death on the jagged rocks. He looks up to heaven and shouts out; 'If there's anybody up there, please help me.' A voice from Heaven replies, 'Just trust in me, let go of the branch and I will catch you in my arms.' After a short pause, the man looks up again and says, 'Is there anybody else up there?'

All too often people give up on their belief in God because God has not come up to expectations. Prayers go unanswered, innocent people suffer, religion becomes unhelpful or the experience of God simply disappears when it is most needed. But if we accept from the outset that our picture of God is incomplete, that it is constructed from, as it were, no more than ripples in the water after a boat has passed by (the evidence of something as yet unseen), then, when God fails to deliver, we can review our picture of God rather than necessarily throwing out the whole idea. In the 11th century, St Anselm constructed an argument (the ontological argument) for proof of the existence of God. It ran something like this:

God (by definition) is that than which nothing greater can be thought. Yet that which actually exists (has substance) is greater than that which only exists in the mind through thought. It follows then that if God is the greatest thing that can be thought, and that actual existence is greater than thought, God must actually exist. Or put more simply, actual being is greater than mere thought. God is the greatest thing we can think of; therefore God must actually exist.

I agree that this is something of a mind-bender, but it is a neat proposition, and philosophers have argued about it from that day to this, and logically it works. But logic doesn't take us very far. Neither God nor anything else can be argued into existence if it does not already exist. Anybody who wants proof of the existence of God is going to come unstuck, at least if the sort of proof required is concrete, tangible and incontrovertible.

Yet there are other aspects of life whose existence is just as difficult to prove, but which we do take for granted. Love and hate, beauty and ugliness are facts of life we live with on a daily basis. Yet we are no more able to prove their objective existence than we can prove God's existence.

Love and beauty, hatred and ugliness are experienced as existential reality, not just by the individual, but cojectively by the whole of humanity. It's certainly true that any particular description of these notions won't be universally accepted, but the underlying truth that love and beauty, as well as hatred and ugliness do indeed exist, is taken for granted by most of us. It is the fact that we experience these things, and that the experience is shared by others, that makes them 'realities' for us. It seems to me that if we're prepared to accept the existence of love without there being any objective reality outside ourselves, then, by the same criteria, there's no reason to dismiss the existence of God.

I have my own 'proof' of God's existence which, rather than being based on logic, is based on everyday experience. It works as follows: love and beauty, we know from experience, do exist; however, they cannot be proven either to exist or not to exist; therefore, that which is known but cannot be proven to exist or not to exist, does, our cojective experience tells us, actually exist. God is known through experience to exist, but cannot be proven either to exist or not to exist. Therefore, using the same criteria as we do for love and beauty, God does actually exist.

I hope we've already agreed that this form of argument from experience cannot prove the actual and objective existence of God. What it does do, though, is to prove (to my satisfaction at least) that God is at least as real as love and beauty. As love and beauty and other cojective experiences are things that give life much of its meaning, we can also say that God, through the cojective experience of humanity, actually exists – at least to the same extent that most meaningful realities in human life exist.

So if it is as reasonable to believe in God as it is to believe in love and beauty, what sort of being is it that we can believe in? Well,

I guess that if I'm being true to what I said earlier in this chapter, I cannot speak in universal terms, but rather must paint a 'picture' that is personal to me. My hope, though, is that since cojectively we have a shared experience of God, my 'picture' will resonate with you, for perhaps you bought this book in the first place because your 'picture' of God doesn't gel with the religious stereotype. I fully accept that my 'picture' of God won't suit everybody, and to some it will seem a rejection of traditional teaching. Be that as it may, I offer my 'picture', not because I wish to persuade others that I've got it right, but simply as an alternative perception. And there must be room for alternative perceptions because, if God exists at all, and if God is infinite (as traditional formulations claim), then it must mean that as finite beings it is impossible to have anything other than a partial and incomplete perception. By definition, the infinite cannot be known by the finite.

So: what sort of a being? The key to my understanding is that God is not a being at all. To think of God as a being, no matter what descriptive phrases we use, such as infinite (can *a* being be infinite?), omnipresent, omniscient etc, is to make God into one being among others.

At our daughter's nativity play many years ago, the children sang a few of their favourite songs. In one the line ran, 'My God is so big, so strong and so mighty, there's nothing he cannot do.' During the singing, the children made the appropriate gestures, flexing their muscles to show how strong God is. Of course, along with other parents, I loved it, my heart melting like butter on a summer's day. But as children grow into teenagers, and teenagers into adults, the idea that God is so big, strong and mighty that 'there is nothing he cannot do', doesn't square with reality – with famine, for example, or starvation and mass death. Such a being is either not so strong and mighty after all, or the way in which he chooses to operate leaves much to be desired.

When one looks at the world, both historically and right now, it's easy to conclude that if God is such a mighty being and somehow 'in charge', then he hasn't made a very good fist of things, and that his morality is more than a little wayward. But what if we delete the single word 'a' and talk of God not as a being, but simply as *Being*. This is far more difficult to grasp; a being has attributes we can talk about, but just Being – how do you begin to describe that? Well you can't, of course, and from my point of view, that suggests we're more likely to be on the right track because, as I say, it isn't possible for the finite to know or describe the infinite.

I realise that God as pure Being is not a comfortable thought; it negates the sort of relationship that is possible with 'a being'; it makes the idea of prayer much harder (more about that later), and it removes the possibility that 'our' God is the only 'right' god to worship. Yet while the concept of God as pure Being is less tangible, and reduces our levels of certainty, it also opens up new possibilities that are denied us when we're limited by the idea of God being a particular being. God as Being is a unifying experience. Regardless of how we choose to worship God (or not), whatever religious path we tread (or don't), God as Being becomes the *highest* common denominator for all of creation.

We all share our being with Being itself. In other words, all things and people who exist (or have being) do so by the very fact of Being. Without Being we would cease to exist. So God as Being necessarily breaks down barriers. There's also a sense of unity for the individual, a sense spoken of by the mystics of all religions, and an insight that's true for primitive pagan beliefs. We are truly at one with the whole cosmos simply because we're 'being' together. God as Being is, at one and the same time, completely other than ourselves, but also supremely personal, the core of my very own being. The difference between understanding God as a being or as Being is, for me, like the difference between being in love and actually loving.

When we fall in love with another person the experience is dynamic – let me call it a 'white water experience'. We cannot get enough of the other person and our ardour is great (sexual ardour and religious ardour are not as far apart as you might imagine). But how much do we actually love the other person? Is it not a projection, an image that we're in love with? At the beginning of a relationship we know very little about the actual person we've fallen in love with; rather we love what that person represents for us. Only given a great deal of time do we begin to know what the other person really is like. The divorce rate is so high in Britain and other western countries simply because people marry an image that seldom matches the reality.

Unless couples are prepared for the hard work of getting to know each other, and loving that person instead of clinging to the image, then the partnership is doomed. But when we do let go of the image, that projection of our own wants and needs, and really love the other person for whom he or she is, instead of who we want them to be, then the relationship is transformed. Gone is the white water exhilaration and not bearing to be separated for a moment; replacing it is love that is like deep still water of unfathomable depth.

So for love, so for God. Understanding God as a being is to project our own wants and needs, to grasp at an image that may or may not match our expectations. Relating to God as Being, however, is to release our projections and enter into the deep mystery of Being itself. My being in total Being. As with a loving human relationship that develops and deepens over time, language is too crude a tool to express the depth of integration one feels. But such a depth, which from the outside can look tepid when compared with the violence of 'being in love', is where the human heart connects at its most profound level. But reaching this point won't be possible if we cling single-mindedly to an image we've created in our own minds, to satisfy our own needs.

God understood as Being in its fullest sense is completely personal. God is known, but not as we know an object, a chair or a bicycle. That is simply to know *about* something; there is no communication between person and object – we can know about an object, but it can never know us. Only people can experience communal cojectivity – being known by that which we know. Life is given meaning not through things, possessions, but through the meeting of the hearts and minds of two persons.

God as a being becomes another object onto which we project our hopes and fears. We know about this God only because we created 'him' in the beginning. But God as Being is experienced both supremely by me at the centre of my own being, and also as otherness, the source of all being. God can never be known as an object because objects cannot be known, only known about. It is a paradox, a mystery. But life is full of such mysteries.

This paradox is experienced by lovers in the act of making love – not just having sex, but making love. In the physical giving by two persons of one to the other, and especially at the point of orgasm, each is both, at one and the same time, self-fulfilled and also fully at one with the other person. So it is with God as Being, we are at one with ourselves, and at one with the source of all Being. For me, then, God is real and God is personal because the most real things in life are not objects to be known about, but persons with whom cojective experiences are shared.

In a marvellous interview given on BBC television's 'Face to Face' series many years ago, Carl Jung the psychiatrist and psychoanalyst was asked the question, 'Do you now believe in God?' After some moments of reflection, Jung, who was by no means conventionally religious replied, 'No... I do not need to believe. I know.'

In the cojective activity of humankind, God as Being is simply present; belief is unnecessary because every single human being experiences Being in and through their own being in the world. Whether or not we choose to give Being the name 'God' matters not a jot, for Being will be, and we will share in it, regardless of the name we use to describe it.

Some may object and say that I am not describing God at all, just the experience of being human. Well, yes, of course. I am a human being, and my experience is that of being human, which I share with other humans, and the language I use is human. Yet humans have, from the beginning of recorded history, struggled to express their feelings of knowing and being known, and that behind our being is greater Being.

I can say no more than this: that along with other human beings I imbibe, cojectively, meaning that extends far beyond the bounds of objective matter. Love, which has no material substance, is more real to me than the car I drive around in (and in a few years my car will cease to exist). In the same way, I experience my being as part of greater Being, and like love, it gives meaning to my life. This Being I choose to call God.

We used to worship together, Betty and I, in pretty traditional ways (sadly, like Joan Hickson, Betty died a few years ago). What we were affirming wasn't that we believed in a being 'out there' somewhere, but rather that life had meaning for us, and that this meaning is shared with others cojectively, so that we have our being in Being itself. We are united in the Spirit of Being where meaning finds its ultimate source. Whatever we choose to call God, God will always remain a profound mystery; but what we experience will always be more real than any object ever can be.

'God,' said St John, 'is love', and love is the cojective experience of humanity which gives meaning to life. Love is a state of being, and Being is what we call God. In the end it is simplicity itself.

As human beings our aim must be to live and share a life of love, for love gives us meaning and purpose. We need not speculate on the nature of God, nor even bother to argue about God's existence. Love is our contact point; when true love is shared between human beings, then we experience something of the divine, and God is seen on earth.

# CHAPTER 9

## 'Hello wall'

"Hi ya wall." So starts the film version of Willy Russell's *Shirley Valentine*. Shirley, a 42-year-old Liverpool housewife, converses with 'wall'. It is 'wall' she complains to, 'wall' she confides in, and 'wall' she shares her glass of wine with. When her husband, Joe, arrives home to find her talking to the wall, he thinks she's going round the bend.

One working definition of madness, of course, is losing touch with reality, and many would argue that wall-talking is just that (although given Shirley's mind-numbing existence, such behaviour could well be her sanest option). Which brings me round to this thought: what's the difference between talking to a wall and prayer? The atheist would say there's no difference, except that if you're talking to a wall at least *something* is there, whereas prayer finds you talking to a will-o'-the-wisp fantasy.

Yet for the religious of all persuasions, billions of them worldwide, prayer is, if not a daily occurrence, something they engage in regularly. Even Buddhists, who don't subscribe to a god as such, practise what looks very much like prayer to many believers in God. So what are those who pray actually doing? Is it all delusional? Are we all 'loop-the-loop' like Shirley Valentine? Is there room for 'prayer' in the life of the non-believer, the life of those who wish to claim a spiritual dimension without claiming a religious affiliation?

Let's start this particular inquiry with the traditional notion of prayer – an individual or group talking (not necessarily aloud) to God, an all-powerful being in Heaven who listens to the prayers of 'his' devotees and answers them. Sometimes, the faithful believe, their wishes are granted, sometimes denied, and sometimes answered in ways they didn't expect. By this reckoning, God always answers prayers for the best, because he knows what is good for his children.

The uncommitted observer will note that, by this formulation, God cannot lose: whatever happens, good or bad, God has responded appropriately. In many ways there seems to be little difference between this and random chance. The non-believer will attribute outcomes to the 'luck of the draw', the believer to the 'will of God'.

As I've already made clear, I don't accept the notion of God as an all-powerful being somewhere 'out there' who intervenes in our lives in a random fashion. But let's consider for a moment a few examples of where the blinkered faith and misguided priorities of those who cling to such ideas, leads them.

I have heard Christians say that an ailment as trifling as a cold has been cured by God because they prayed for it. Personally, I am outraged by the idea of a God who would intercede so particularly over a piffling matter like a head cold. If God has that sort of control and power, what on earth is he doing curing some pious Christian's sniffles while leaving millions of famine victims to starve on the other side of the world?

My wife Ruth is an ordained priest in the Church of England, and when, in November 1992, the General Synod voted to ordain women into the priesthood, nobody was more delighted than I. But I have to say that the fuss the Church has made about it, and continued to make until 2014 about the ordination of women bishops, the obvious and logical next step, makes me heartily sick. God has been bombarded with prayers and masses and vigils from those on both sides of the divide. Prayers for the will of God to be done, and for the guidance of the Holy Spirit, have been directed Heavenward for years.

For so many people in the Church of England and other churches, trying to discern the 'will of God' consumes huge amounts of time and energy. Apart from the simple justice implicit in granting women an equal right to exercise their gifts and responsibilities, which is certainly an issue for all of us, I cannot believe that a God worth his salt cares tuppence about the ordination of women (or men come to that). A God who concerns himself with theological niceties and doctrinal correctness while half his human creation starves or tears itself apart in bloody conflict, seems to me as irrational as it is offensive.

In October 1917, when the Russian Revolution began and much of human history was knocked onto a new trajectory, many millions died and many more suffered great hardship. However, a traditional story has it, the Russian Church chose that moment to assemble in council, the passions of delegates running high as arguments were flung back and forth. The subject? The colour of their liturgical vestments... Should they be white or purple?

The concerns of the Church, and therefore the subjects of its prayers, are often so parochial that God is perceived as acting more like a company boss trying to keep the show on the road than with the merits and wholeness of creation itself. If God is such a being, responding to prayers in the way many Christians often suppose, and if his focus is largely on religious liturgy, then, quite frankly, I'd rather talk to Shirley's wall.

In the previous chapter, I conceded that thinking about God as Being, rather than as a being, makes prayer more difficult. No longer is there a figurehead, a Big Daddy, with whom to communicate. We cannot expect answers in the same way once God is understood to be the one Being in which we all have our own being.

In times of conflict a Big Daddy God instantly becomes tribal. In the Hebrew Scriptures, there are countless references to the God of Israel lording it over the gods of the Hittites, the Amorites, the Canaanites and so on. In modern times it is no less so. When the United Kingdom was in conflict with Argentina over the Falkland Islands/Malvenas, prayers beseeching victory were offered up by both sides. Since both countries are, nominally at least, Christian, both were applying to the same God for his favour. Where's the sense in that?

God as Being cannot be recruited to a specific cause, can never be partisan, but will be understood and generously accepted as being just as much the God of the enemy as the God of patriots. God is no longer a 'doer' who intervenes in the world, but is rather the totality of all being and all action, for without Being itself, nothing else would or could be. This makes prayer as an activity extremely difficult. Not only is there no 'person' to talk to, but what could reasonably be asked of him/her anyway? Because God as an interventionist cuts no ice, petition and intercession (asking for oneself and others) is useless (if we are expecting answers), as is thanksgiving. Certainly being thankful is no bad thing, but can we really give thanks to God for specific acts of goodness on our behalf?

A person who survives a plane crash may give thanks to God for his survival, but what is he giving thanks for? Surely no one could believe that God had intervened to save him personally, while allowing others to perish? To believe that God especially intervenes to bless or save some people while allowing, or even worse causing, the downfall of others, is beyond my comprehension. Such a being would certainly not be God, but a god, and if I'm going to invest time and energy in prayer, then I need to feel that I'm not wasting it talking to an imagined deity who has even less substance than Shirley Valentine's 'wall'.

But if prayer is not an activity, what is it? I want to suggest that it is a way of being, and has much to do with *who* we are, but little (except incidentally) with what we do. That is not to say we don't also need to 'do' prayer as a particular activity, either to learn the way of being prayerful or as an aide-mémoire to continued practice. If one thinks of a child learning to write, in the early stages it's very much an activity in itself and goes no further than the learning of shapes. Slowly these shapes take on significance as combinations of them begin to represent words, then sentences. By the time the art of writing has been thoroughly learned, writing itself becomes second nature and the means by which communication takes place.

As an activity, prayer is like learning to write – something we do at certain times and so learn the art of simply being prayerful. As an activity it doesn't have to mean that we're directing our prayers to another being (God out there), but that we're reminding ourselves of a way of living our lives that is beyond just ourselves. Prayer is traditionally regarded as talking and listening to God. But let me rephrase that: prayer is allowing my being to be in tune with Being itself. Whether we conceive of Being in theistic terms, or in terms of the wholeness of creation, doesn't greatly matter. How we choose to define Being will affect our practice and beliefs; what it will not do is affect the reality of Being itself.

So what is a prayerful person? To return to our writing analogy, one wouldn't describe a writer as someone who practises writing, but rather as someone who communicates through the written word. The physical act of writing (or typing) is by-the-by, the means not the end. A prayerful person is, I want to suggest, not someone who spends her or his time in the actual act of prayer, but someone who lives life with a quality of awareness of themselves, of others, and of the environment.

75

In other words, a prayerful person is the woman or man who, in their daily life, is aware of their part in, and responsibility to, Being itself.

By this definition a great many people could be called prayerful who aren't in the least religious. By the same token, many piously religious people are anything but prayerful. If we can get away from the notion that prayer is like talking to a being who can zap our hang-nails if only we pray earnestly enough, we can (to return to our earlier analogy), stop practising writing and start to use it for the business of living our lives to the full.

I am no carpenter – it took me an entire term at school to make a simple teapot stand – yet I do know that it's easier to work with the grain of the wood than against it. Nor am I a great swimmer, but I do know that swimming with the current is easier and more productive than trying to swim against it. When we become people of prayer (secular or religious), what we're trying to do is become aware of, and go with, the flow of life, the flow of Being.

Meditation is now practised widely in non-religious settings because it is understood to help people function more healthily. Those who are aware of themselves, aware of others and of the Being of life, are more able to go with the flow, to feel at one with their fellows and all creation. At one level prayer is a selfish thing because it frees us to live more creatively; but creativity, like ripples in a pond, spreads outward, affecting all it comes into contact with. The more creative we can be, the better for all.

I may know little about carpentry, and even less about modem physics, yet chaos theory resonates within me. If the flapping of a butterfly's wings in England, can, by the ripple effect, eventually cause a tropical storm on the other side of the world, then every action is interlinked with every other to produce either cumulative good or cumulative evil.

Prayer is effective, therefore, not because we ask a deity to intervene in our affairs, but because it changes our very being into something that more fully represents pure Being itself. Prayer, or at least an attitude of prayer, does actually change things. It isn't just talking to the wall, even if it can be a therapeutic thing to do. Nor is it simply a release for those with extroverted temperaments; rather it's an attitude of being that actively seeks the goal of union. Like those pond ripples it works outwards. First we need to feel united within ourselves and at peace with who we are. Secondly, we need to feel harmony with our fellows and embrace our common humanity. And thirdly, as those ripples extend, we need to understand our place within, and our unity with, all of creation, so that it becomes impossible for us consciously to abuse either the animal world or the environment. Increasingly prayer becomes, not so much an activity in which we are involved – although it may be that as well – but a way of being and relating, first to other beings, and then to Being itself.

But prayer isn't only about being and becoming. I have personally been involved in prayer that has led to physical change and healing. I don't believe that God was intervening from 'on high', but rather it was the cumulative effect of people attempting to get in tune with the flow of Being itself, and that, when the flow of life is enabled rather than thwarted, things actually do happen. If humankind, whatever the religious persuasion of individuals (or the absence thereof), were to start to live prayerfully, that is to discern and go with the flow of Being itself, then we'd see a transformation in this world that is beyond our wildest imagining.

For those wanting to live a spiritual life, regardless of religious affiliation, prayer is an essential element. It is a discipline we need to embrace if we want to make the journey towards becoming who we really are, before becoming one with Being itself. How we externally express such discipline will differ between individuals. What's important, if we're not to create yet greater divisions and go against the flow, is to understand that prayer isn't primarily an activity that's easily recognised from the outside, but rather a way of being that takes many forms.

I know people of prayer who would hate to be thought of as religious; I also know highly religious people who, by my definition, seem never to have been prayerful in their lives. Being a prayerful person is much harder, and involves more, than just settling down to pray. It demands that we focus our entire being, all of the time, in the direction of unity with all beings and with Being itself.

A saying of Jesus that's often interpreted in narrowly Christian terms, talks about the way of prayerfulness:

> 'In everything, do to others as you would have them do
> to you; for this is the law of the prophets.
> Enter through the narrow gate; for the gate is wide and

the road is easy that leads to destruction, and there are many who take it. For the gate is narrow and the road is hard that leads to life, and there are few who find it. Beware of false prophets, who come to you in sheep's clothing but inwardly are ravenous wolves. You will know them by their fruits. Are grapes gathered from thorns, or figs from thistles? In the same way every good tree bears good fruit, but a bad tree bears bad fruit. A good tree cannot bear bad fruit, nor can a bad tree bear good fruit. Every tree that does not bear good fruit is cut down and thrown into the fire. Thus you will know them by their fruits.' (Matthew 7:12-20)

The discipline of a life of prayerfulness is hard indeed; it runs contrary to the selfishness, greed and narrow-mindedness of our materialistic society, where things – objects – are loved and people are used. The gate is narrow, not because it is limited to one particular religious tradition, but because it follows the path of love and compassion, something that seems in short supply in our world. Remember, Jesus said 'you will know them by their fruits'.

People who live prayerful lives, be they religious or not, can be identified 'by their fruits'. Prayerful living is integrated living, and it makes a difference that is tangible. For anyone trying to live a spiritual life, prayer is not an optional extra, it is an attitude of being and becoming that is central to the endeavour. The danger lies in narrowing our perception of prayer so that it becomes a particular activity that is exclusive rather than inclusive. Prayer is much more than talking to 'wall'; it is also much more than religion often portrays it as being. Try it, and go with the flow.

# CHAPTER 10

## And then there were three

This chapter almost didn't happen. Chapters 11, 12 and 13 were written before it. I found reasons enough to leave it out, most of them unworthy: I could get the book published sooner without it; nobody would notice if it wasn't there. But the more I tried to justify its exclusion, the more it nagged me. In the introduction I claim that if nothing else this will be an honest book, and I knew that if I avoided writing this chapter I would be being less than honest, certainly with myself.

My reluctance can be sourced to the sheer difficulty of the subject matter – the Christian doctrine of the Trinity. Over the centuries, reams have been written to explain and elucidate this most difficult of concepts. God – three in one. There is nothing in the Bible that addresses the Trinity explicitly; rather the doctrine was created by the early Church which drew on implicit references. Some, I have to say, are particularly dubious. The 'sanctus' from Isaiah 6:3 is one such: **'And one called to another and said: "Holy, holy, holy is the Lord of hosts; the whole earth is full of his glory."'**

To start with, accepting a vision as an objective description of God seems especially doubtful. But even then, the fact that the seraphs say 'holy, holy, holy' is hardly evidence of God as three-in-one. One might as well say that a policeman asking, ''Ello, 'ello, 'ello, what's going on 'ere then?' is proof that he has nabbed a trinitarian villain.

But I don't intend, here, to itemise biblical evidence, nor do I plan to detail the process by which the Church formulated the doctrine of the Trinity. That has been exhaustively covered elsewhere.

What I will ask is whether the doctrine of the Trinity makes any sense experientially – what in our lives and experience supports an understanding of God as three-in-one?

The idea of God as a Trinity comes unstuck, of course, when we try to conceive of such a Trinity actually existing 'out there' somewhere. It's a problem common to all doctrines – an attempt to pin down a spiritual concept in concrete terms. A doctrine pushes the cojective into the objective, and in so doing transforms the original meaning utterly. The phrase 'my love is like a red, red rose' is not an objective statement, but is understood cojectively; the hearer knows what the speaker means because it's an idiom we all recognise and share. Taken literally, it would be pretty meaningless. So, too, equivalent talk of the Trinity becomes meaningless if we try to think of it in literal terms. Rather, for those who believe in God, and those who believe Jesus revealed something of the Divine (more about this in Part 2), the Trinity is a poetic expression of ultimate values and experiences. Primarily, though, it is about relationships, and I ask you to bear with me here as I appear to digress.

If, as I suggested in Chapter 8, God is not a being, but Being itself, then relationships and integration must, in the very nature of things, be constituent parts. Being without relationships and integration, human or otherwise, could not exist at all, because nothing would hang together. Both science and ecology point increasingly to the fact that the world we live in, indeed the entire cosmos, is an interrelated construct; only too slowly are we learning that we simply cannot continue to misuse and abuse our environment without suffering long-term, often unexpected and probably appalling consequences. To be healthy there must be balance in the world; this is true not only for individuals, but for families, groups, communities and nations. Without proper balance everything suffers.

For an individual there needs to be a balance in such everyday matters as diet, work and leisure, waking and sleep... Unless relationships between all such things are right, then ill-health, physical, mental or psychological, may well follow. And what is true for us as individuals, is true on a global scale, as well as in every sub-division between. We will never be truly happy, truly whole, while we in industrialised nations discard more food than many nations ever have. We shall never be whole while the earth's natural resources continue to be exploited for short-term gain. A spiritual view of the world must be a holistic view, recognising the interdependence of all things, a view long held not least, for example, by the 17th-century poet and cleric John Donne:

> 'No man is an island entire of itself…/ Any man's death diminishes me, / Because I am involved in mankind, / And therefore never send to know for whom the bell tolls; / It tolls for thee.'

One of the tragedies of modern Western society is the breakdown of community. Much of the suffering we endure today is directly caused by our increasing isolation. We no longer know who our neighbours are. Families live insular lives, not only separated from other family members, often by many miles or even continents; and individual families, although living under one roof, can also be fragmented. The days when they would talk together over family meals, play games and actually communicate are gone, and so, even, is the time when the family would gather round the television together.

In Britain today the average home has multiple television sets and other screens of various sorts, and family members spend increasing time doing their own thing, or, more to the point, watching their own programme or playing their own game. I'm not against family members pursuing personal interests, it's part of that important life balance, but I do believe that it becomes profoundly unhealthy when people no longer have either the time or inclination to communicate even within their own family structures. We learn who we are, what value we have, not in isolation, but in relationship with others. I know that I am loved and accepted – the most important thing anybody needs to know – not by looking in the mirror, and certainly not from watching television or going on-line, but by seeing it in the eyes of another human being. So much of the pain, the violence, the mindless destruction that contaminates our modern culture, can be directly connected to people feeling worthless and unloved. If I feel that I have no value as a person, if I feel unloved and unlovable, then it becomes impossible for me to love and respect another person. I can give only as much as I receive. Love is a language.

Many popular songs speak about the 'language of love', but if I have never learned that language in the first place, I can hardly expect to speak it. I am dyslexic; as a child at school in the 1950s and early '60s, dyslexia was neither known about nor understood. I could not read to the same standard as my peers, could never spell (and still cannot, so thank goodness for the word processor), and had, and have, very little facility for remembering certain things.

With the exception of one teacher at my secondary school, who I shall always be grateful to for the respect he paid me as an individual, I was mostly ridiculed and/or punished. Needless to say, that didn't improve my dyslexia, so I spent a great deal of time bunking off, and in my primary school days the 'school board man' as he was then known, was a constant visitor to my home. The punishments that then followed simply drove me further from the help and acceptance I needed.

Punishment is no answer for the crime and violence so prevalent in our society today; it treats a symptom, the cause of which is deep spiritual malaise. I'm not saying that symptoms don't need to be treated, but it seems that only a society that is itself sick would want to punish those who are victims of that very same sickness. No one would dream of punishing a person for not being able to speak a language they've never come across, yet we expect unloved people to show respect, love, tolerance and understanding towards others when it's a 'language' they've never learned.

Rich and affluent societies nevertheless contain millions upon millions of deprived children (I'm not just talking about those who come from poor homes and slums or ghettos, although of course many of those do suffer terribly). Physical deprivation is just one symptom of a sick society, but the deprivation I'm concerned with here is spiritual deprivation – the deprivation born of insufficient and inadequate relationships. There are no class boundaries to this kind of deprivation, no financial limits, no material dividing lines. Some of the most deprived people I have come across in my work as a psychotherapist have been individuals from privileged wealthy and even upper-class backgrounds. The deprivation is spiritual, not material.

Experiments with monkeys (the ethics of which I shall leave for another day) carried out by Harlow and Suomi in 1970 proved conclusively that when raised with artificial mothers these lab monkeys showed an innate preference for a soft and warm substitute 'mother' to one that simply supplied food. But the most illuminating of the experimental results emerged when the monkeys grew to adulthood.

Infant monkeys raised with artificial mothers and isolated from other monkeys during the first six months of life showed various types of bizarre behaviour in adulthood. They rarely engaged in normal interaction with other monkeys later on... and their sexual response was inappropriate. When female monkeys that were deprived of early social contact were successfully mated (after considerable effort), they made very poor mothers, tending to neglect or abuse their infants. [2]

Work on attachment issues by psychologist Ronald Bowlby has also shown that what is true for monkeys is equally true for human beings:

The failure to form attachment to one or a few primary persons in the early years can be related to an inability to develop close personal relationships in adulthood. [3]

Forming close personal relationships is the one crucial factor common to the development of healthy people, because an abundance of material wealth can be as detrimental to good relationships as an oppressive lack of material necessity. In short, there is no substitute for loving and accepting relationships. A relationship means actually knowing and being known, not knowing *about* someone or them knowing *about* us, which is simply knowledge of subject to object; knowing *about* is not relationship.

It is this vital spiritual element of which our modern society is so bereft. It shows in our materialism, our rushing after time, our greed to possess. We have lost, or are at least in danger of losing, that most precious of human gifts, our spiritual nature, our cojective ability to be at one with one another, and with the environment upon which we depend. We could learn a lot from the following contented fisherman...

A rich businessman from London was horrified to find a Cornish fisherman lying lazily beside his boat, smoking his pipe.
'Why aren't you out fishing?' said the businessman.

---

[2] Psychology, 9th edition, Atkinson, Atkinson, Smith & Hilgard (1985)
[3] Bowlby (1973)

'Because I have caught enough fish for the day,' said the fisherman.

'Why don't you catch more?'

'Why would I want to catch more? What would I do with them?'

'You could earn more money' was the reply. 'With that you could have a motor fixed to your boat and go further out and catch more fish. Then you could make enough money to buy new nylon nets. These would bring you more fish and more money. Soon you would have enough money to own two boats... maybe eventually, even a whole fleet of boats. Then you would be rich like me.'

'What would I do then?'

'Then you could really enjoy life.'

'What do you think I'm doing right now?'

In our headlong rush to find happiness in material wealth, a happiness we're constantly bombarded with by advertising, posters and glossy magazines, we have lost sight of our real treasure – human relationships. Jesus said:

> 'Do not store up for yourselves treasures on earth, where moth and rust consume and where thieves break in and steal; but store up for yourselves treasure in heaven, where neither moth nor rust consumes and where thieves do not break in and steal. For where your treasure is, there your heart will be also.' (Matthew 6:19)

That is a profound spiritual truth; where your treasure is, there will your heart be also. If our treasure is found in objects, with which we can have no relationship, then our heart will be there also, bereft of the most vital of all human needs.

We therefore need not be surprised by the violence and greed in society at large; material gain is where our heart is. Unless and until, in all layers of society, from poorest to richest, priority is given to loving and caring relationships, especially among the young, we will continue to suffer all the symptoms of a sick society, punishing offenders for doing only what they have been taught to do – putting their heart where their treasure is – in objects, not in people.

All of which may seem a long diversion from the doctrine of the Trinity, but I believe it is central to it. Trinity is about Being in relationship. Whatever the objective truth of God is (something we can never know), what the Christian understanding brings us is that ultimate Being, be it human or divine, does not operate in isolation. At the core of creation is a relationship that overflows with creative love. The Holy Spirit – always regarded as the feminine aspect of God – is the very spirit of human cojectivity that flows between people as the creative and unifying power of love. The experience of the early Church, their understanding of Jesus and the cojective experience of the Spirit, led to the formulation of the doctrine of the Trinity – Father, Son and Holy Spirit. But we need not regard these words as descriptive of three actual beings, but rather as symbolic of the interdependent relationship at the heart of Being itself.

We cannot live a spiritual existence outside true relationships, both with others, and with our environment. Many psychological illnesses would not exist if people enjoyed genuine loving relationships. Conflicts and wars would be far less likely to occur if people really knew one another, for so much conflict is based on ignorance and prejudice. Nor would we rape the very earth upon whose existence we depend if our relationship with it was more respectful.

The doctrine of the Trinity then is central to spiritual understanding, not because it speaks of an objective reality in which we must believe, but because it points to the essential nature of creation – the interdependence in relationships.

# CHAPTER 11

## Divine eternity

The idea of eternity, life after death, is as old as humankind. Every civilisation has had its own concept of a life after this one, often involving elaborate preparation (by those rich and powerful enough) for the journey into the hereafter. Today, though, there are basically three differing sets of beliefs.

First, that nothing at all lies beyond our physical death. The human spirit is understood to be inextricably at one with the mechanics and chemistry of our brain and nervous system. When the 'machine' stops, that's it. It's a view deserving serious thought because, scientifically speaking, the evidence looks compelling. Although many have endured near-death experiences (I'll have more to say about that shortly) there is nothing to indicate, beyond anecdote and belief, that life outstrips physical oblivion. I should add, though, that while there is no scientific evidence in support of immortality, there is no actual proof, either, that there is no afterlife.

The second form of belief about our post-mortem existence comes from the Christian, Jewish and Moslem traditions. Within Christianity, although the belief seems uniform from the outside, there are in fact differing beliefs drawing on a single theme. The central idea concerns continuing life when, after departing this world, the individual is 'judged'. Depending on how well or badly we have behaved, we may either go straight to Heaven (without passing Go), or to Hell and everlasting torment in fire and brimstone.

Large sections of Christianity also believe in Purgatory, a sort of half-way house where those not considered good enough to go straight to Heaven can work off their sins before being allowed through the pearly gates. Although fewer people believe in a heaven of clouds, harps and wings in this day and age, and even fewer in a hell of brimstone and fire, they are still conceived of as final destinations after death, even if the details are less lurid than they once were. It is supposed that in Heaven we'll enjoy everlasting life in the presence of God and the company of the saints. Hell, if it's considered at all nowadays, is often portrayed as a grey and lonely locale drenched in isolation and despair. However they're pictured, this view of the afterlife is one of eternal existence in another place.

The third belief system is that of reincarnation or transmigration of the soul. (Reincarnation is the movement of the soul from one human body to another; transmigration is the movement to or from any life form – human, animal or vegetable – to another.) This view is held predominantly in the East, particularly by the Hindu and Buddhist faiths. The belief is that the soul (*atman*) passes after death into another being, and it may happen thousands of times. The point of reincarnation is that the soul continues to acquire greater wisdom as it passes from incarnation to incarnation, eventually achieving enlightenment (an end point that differs for Hindus and Buddhists).

In Hinduism, where there is a belief in God, enlightenment leads to the individual soul, the *atman*, being reunited with supreme Being, Brahman, from which it emerged in the first place. In Buddhism, where there is no God, the goal of enlightenment is to escape the continual cycle of birth and re-birth (*samsara*), and enter Nirvana, a sort of beingless bliss. (Nirvana is a state that Buddhists themselves usually decline to describe, but 'beingless bliss', I think, points in the right direction.)

From the two basic sets of beliefs accounting for post-mortem life – Heaven and Hell, or reincarnation – many variations arise. Reincarnation does not preclude Heaven and Hell; in Hinduism they are understood to be 'stop-off points' between lives, and Buddhism certainly entertains the idea of other levels of existence beyond this world. While in Christianity, although the official line has always been one of resurrection and Heaven, reincarnation is what many practising Christians actually believe.

In our pluralist society, in which ideas from all the great religions have been circulating freely for more than 200 years, and certainly since the turn of the 20th century, we now also have pick 'n' mix beliefs among people of all faiths and none. So what can we reasonably believe about life after death?

Part of the problem, it seems to me, is that it is equally reasonable to believe any of the above. The question is, do any of these beliefs actually affect the way we live our lives here and now? Let's look first at the first belief itemised above, or perhaps I should say non-belief. If I believe there is nothing after this life, how might that influence me now?

Well, firstly, there would be no consequences – neither fear of punishment nor hope of reward. What you see is what you get. It may be thought that this rather bleak outlook would perhaps spur people to live a selfish, self-centred existence. An individual might say, 'If this is all there is, let's make the most of it. I'll take all I can while I can, and to hell with anyone who gets in my way.'

That may be true for some, but history seems to suggest that when people really did believe in Heaven and Hell, their behaviour was no better than it is today. In fact, some of the worst atrocities inflicted man upon man, have been committed by those who thought they had Heaven on their side. The Crusades, the Inquisition and at the time of writing, the so-called 'Islamic State', are all examples of men (and it generally is *men*) who like to claim they are somehow doing 'God's will'. They can *claim* anything they like, of course, but that doesn't negate the fact that some are simply deluded or disingenuous or plain psychopathic killers, using 'God' as a prop or an excuse. No, lack of belief in the hereafter doesn't necessarily trigger antisocial behaviour; in fact, the opposite may be true. If I believe that this is all there is, then there is surely a great incentive to make the most of my life, not only for my own satisfaction, but for those with whom I share it. My immortality will rest only in those things marked by my own creativity, things that will stand the test of time and enrich my post-mortem reputation. To believe that this life is the only one we have doesn't therefore contaminate a spiritual view of the world; rather it encourages us to live life to the full right now. It is no good putting things off; tomorrow really will be too late. Nor is belief that we cease to be at the point of death an unspiritual view; what it does is concentrate our spiritual life in the here and now, and that can be no bad thing.

The traditional understanding of life after death 'in Heaven' has a carrot-and-stick feel about it: the reward for being good during life on earth is everlasting life in Heaven. Equally, the consequences of bad behaviour or lack of belief are eternal damnation. In short, we may well feel coerced rather than morally inspired – if I live a good life here only because I fear Hell or hope for Heaven, then I'm not leading a truly spiritual life or being creative and good for their own sake. A truly good action does not emerge from fear or reward, but is undertaken for its own sake alone. Therefore, concerns about Heaven and Hell may actually stand between us and living a properly spiritual life.

Reincarnation is believed in by a great number of the world's population, and since the beginning of the 20th century it has become increasingly popular in the West, not least among Christians, as I've already suggested. Central to belief in reincarnation is the law of *karma*, which can be defined as simple cause and effect. No judge will tally up our sins on the day of our death; *karma* works independently of any deity or absence of deity; it's like a set of pan-scales with evil on one side and good on the other. The downside of such a belief is that it can produce an air of fatalism – suffering in this life is attributed to evil committed in a past life, and an individual has to live through their *karma* in order to 'balance the scales'.

In the Eastern tradition, spirituality is understood very much in individual terms, each person needing to balance their own *karma* and tread their own spiritual path. Enlightenment is reached and the wheel of rebirth escaped (*moksa*), not by doing good but by learning detachment. Goodness in itself therefore cannot bring a person closer to enlightenment and escape, for one can be just as attached to good things as to bad.

For me, the spiritual journey is a profoundly mutual one, where interdependence with other people and our environment is essential. To be too concerned with one's own spiritual journey at the expense of social action and interaction is to miss out on the greatest source of spiritual experience, which is loving human interaction.

But what is the evidence for a life after this? Christians might point to the resurrection of Jesus as proof of on-going life (see Chapter 19), but this, it seems to me, is hardly convincing. Firstly, we cannot be at all sure about what happened on that first Easter Day. If one reads the four accounts in the Gospels, the reported facts do not tally. This in itself isn't conclusive evidence against the resurrection – reports written down some time after the event will be expressed differently by each writer, varying things will be remembered and forgotten, and differing points will be emphasised. What we can assert, both from reading the Gospel stories and studying the traditions of the Church, is that Jesus's disciples did believe he rose from the dead. However, that this was a physical resurrection and that his actual crucified body was re-animated, seems highly unlikely, especially given the texts in which he is portrayed as appearing in locked rooms.

But whatever the experience was, it doesn't in itself establish that there is continued life after death for everybody. One swallow doesn't make a summer, nor does one account of resurrection rubber-stamp a universal truth for all humanity. No, as proof of life after death the resurrection accounts provide, in themselves, insufficient evidence to allow us to draw any general conclusions.

The concept of reincarnation offers us considerably more in the way of 'evidence'. True, none of it is either scientifically or legally rigorous, but anecdotal evidence is abundant. Much of it takes the form of memories of lives previously lived, or at least particular facts that are later verified as correct. While it is possible to find alternative explanations for many such accounts, it seems to me that some events are beyond the ken of scientific analysis and that the possibility of reincarnation cannot be dismissed out of hand.

For some the evidence is overwhelming, and they have no doubts about the validity of this Eastern belief. For others the evidence carries no weight whatsoever. Objectively we can neither prove nor disprove the concept's claims to a continued generation unto generation rolling existence. It seems to me that to be dogmatic one way or the other is to push further than the evidence allows. Like resurrection, it is an idea, a belief, that at least seems feasible, and one we can quite reasonably remain open-minded about.

Those who report that they have experienced near-death episodes come from a wide variety of backgrounds and cultures. There are often two aspects to experiences that point to an existence other than the purely physical. The first is the out-of-body experience where the individual reports seeing themselves from a point, usually somewhere above their own bodies (these events usually occur during acute illness where the patient is, to all external observation, very near death or clinically dead). Some of what they describe after regaining consciousness is hard to account for, other than to accept that they were, in fact, outside their own bodies for a period of time.

The second aspect of a near-death experience is often described as a journey along a tunnel before emerging into a place of brilliant light. Frequently the 'dead' person will encounter previously deceased friends or relatives, and also a religious figure, perhaps Jesus, or a Hindu God or holy man, depending on the culture of the individual. In all the accounts I have seen, the universal effect of the experience has been to make the individual concerned quite certain about a life hereafter, which in turn often had a profound effect upon the rest of her or his earthly life. Personally, I am more convinced by the accounts of people witnessing their own resuscitation than I am by the accounts of an afterlife, which may be caused by a severe lack of oxygen to the brain at crucial moments. Again, evidence either way is inconclusive, except to those who have experienced it. Usually they have no doubts.

In the wake of thousands of years of belief, experience and experiment, proof that there is or is not life after this one continues to elude us. All the evidence from all the religions, and I don't discount spiritualism here, doesn't amount to any sort of actual proof. But add it all together and it seems to me that, although it would be foolish to speculate on the exact, or even inexact, nature of life after physical death, it isn't unreasonable to believe that there is some sort of continuance, albeit that it is as incomprehensible to us now as this life is incomprehensible to the foetus in the womb.

For those intending to live this life spiritually, however, life after this one should be of little concern. All too often, especially within the Christian tradition, eternal life equates to everlasting life, something that happens after death. But eternity is very different from something being everlasting. Remember everlasting gobstoppers? Those great ball-bearing-like sweets that filled the mouth and rotted the teeth but never did, of course, last for ever (but for a small boy with a penny to spend it was heaven). In a very real way the penny gobstopper was more eternal than everlasting. It brought a quality to life that wasn't about being long-lasting, but about the moment, living in the moment, making the best of now. Eternity, therefore, should be understood in terms of quality of time, not quantity. This is the nature of eternal life. It's to do with a quality of living in the moment, about who we are now, not what may become of us after we're dead. To live spiritually is to participate in eternity as a quality of being that is timeless.

In his letter to those living in Corinth, St Paul concludes his famous poem to love with these words: **'There are three things that last forever, faith, hope and love, but the greatest of them all is love.' (1 Corinthians 13)** It could be paraphrased as: there are three *eternal qualities*, faith, hope and love, but the greatest of them all is love.

When we speak about something lasting for ever, we speak about time in terms of quantity. 'For ever' is beyond our imagining; it is a quantity of time that just keeps going, a sort of Alice in Wonderland path that rolls out before us, and rolls up behind us as we go. Something lasting for ever is beyond our comprehension, and certainly beyond our experience. Time as a quality, however, is neither beyond our understanding nor our experience. We have all been in situations where 'time has stood still'. Either we're so entranced and delighted that 'hours pass in moments', or we're involved in some horror where hours seem to go by, but the hands on the clock have barely moved.

Eternity is a quality of life in which we are called, as spiritual beings, to share. The practice of faith, hope and love is the means by which, cojectively, eternity is lived and shared with others. Eternal life is therefore not to be anticipated in post-mortem terms, but to be lived out in the here and now with our fellow human beings, and in the environment of the present day.

Whatever awaits us after death – oblivion, resurrection or reincarnation – doesn't seem to me to matter much. If there is life after death, then there is; if there is nothing, then there is nothing. Either way there seems little point in worrying about it. Too many religious people spend their lives mulling over what will happen after they die. What a waste of time! Live life to the full now, in faith and hope and love; after death, what will be will surely be, and no amount of religious hypothesising or speculation will make a jot of difference. In the 'Hail Mary', the prayer runs, 'pray for us sinners now and at the hour of our death'.

Now – this moment in time – and the fact that we shall die, are really the only two absolute certainties. Between now and the hour of our death, it seems only sensible not to count the minutes but to live a quality of life that is truly eternal.

# CHAPTER 12

## What in religion is necessary for the spiritual life?

If you're of a religious bent by inclination or practice, you may be surprised to hear me claim that nothing in your religious calling is actually essential to a full spiritual life. In this chapter I'll be arguing from the Christian perspective, but I believe it'll become clear that what is true for Christianity is equally true for other faiths. As I've already emphasised, religion is a *response* to a spiritual experience and not a *prerequisite*. Another traditional story may help give you a sense of what I mean.

> An explorer returned to his townspeople who were eager to hear about the Amazon. But how could he ever put into words the feelings that had flooded his heart when he first saw exotic tropical flowers and heard the night sounds of the jungle, or sensed the presence of dangerous wild creatures or paddled his canoe down treacherous rapids? So he simply said, 'Go and find out for yourselves.' To help guide them he drew a map of the river, and they pounced on it. They framed it, they erected it in the town hall, and they made stacks of copies. And all who had a copy considered themselves experts on the river, for did they not now know its every turn and bend, how broad it was and how deep, and where the rapids were and where the falls?

And the point is this: although a map is useful, it's no substitute for the real thing and may even discourage us from exploring for ourselves. Like the townspeople, we might fasten onto it, believing that it offers all we need to experience a spiritual adventure; or else the map may tempt us to confine ourselves to well-trodden paths and so fail to search out a trail that is uniquely right for us as we simply follow the crowd.

Our religion is like that map. Some people who, having once familiarised themselves with their formal faith at a rudimentary level, believe it has given them all they need to know. Their religion is practised at arm's length; it's part of the social fabric and in no way impinges on daily life. Others, though, will study the map more closely and make a real attempt to forge their own path. Over the years, of course, the religion map has been interpreted many, many times, so even those who believe they share the same map, may nevertheless find themselves going in different directions. Despite this paradoxical situation, the map is rigidly adhered to, and straying from the path is considered dangerous, perhaps even sinful.

If you've been taught over many years that the map is essential if you're to arrive at your destination, then the idea of letting it go won't come easily. Or, if you've been directionless for a long time and somebody tells you that their map, and their map alone, is the answer to your quest, then either you'll find the suggestion suffocating or the thought of looking elsewhere a risky business. What I'm suggesting in this chapter is that no single religion (map) in itself provides the whole answer, or is even essential to the spiritual life. We may as individuals want to hang on to much of our religious understanding; that's fine. What we need to realise, though, is that while it may be essential for us, it ain't necessarily so for anyone else.

Let's look at some elements from the Christian tradition that may be thought indispensable to our spiritual quest.

One of the great bones of contention for those who were (or still are) opposed to the ordination of women to the priesthood is the celebration of the Eucharist, otherwise known as the Mass, Holy Communion or the Lord's Supper. Many argue that because Jesus was himself a man, those who represent him as president of the Eucharist should be male as well. This seems to ignore the fact that Jesus was also Middle-Eastern, circumcised, unmarried (as far as we know) and apparently, homeless.

Should all priests be the same? But the argument continues because the Eucharist is considered central to the life of a Christian.

So is the Eucharist also an essential ingredient in the spiritual journey? The answer is clearly no. If it were we would immediately exclude most of the world's population. All those women and men of other faiths and none, who live out their spirituality in loving, human and humane ways, have no need of and many have no knowledge of, Eucharistic participation, yet their spirituality is nonetheless real and valid. Let's not forget, either, that thousands of Christians do not participate in the Eucharist as a formal sacrament – the Salvation Army and Quakers, for example. But which Christians would dare suggest that they are somehow substandard? The Eucharist is non-essential to a worthwhile spiritual life.

Surely, though, the Bible must be crucial? Certainly it is accepted by Christians of every denomination and theological persuasion – the common denominator running through a very diverse religion. Yet how common is it? There are many different translations, of varying accuracy. One of the funniest must be an American version of the Living Bible which has Saul going into a cave to 'use the bathroom'. But it isn't translation that causes real problems, but interpretation.

There are as many different interpretations of any given biblical text as there are divisions within Christendom. They range from the pretty outrageous, such as those that some sects use to justify the preoccupations of their founders (which usually include giving a lot of money to their so-called church), to the orthodoxies of Rome and the East, where tradition has long dictated interpretation.

But even within orthodox Christian denominations where long tradition and sound scholarship have ensured a stable approach, different theologians have interpreted passages in different ways. The Bible is a record of previous people's encounters with God which can, like any tool, be used or abused, and so help or hinder us on our spiritual journey. Jehovah's Witnesses use biblical authority to deny their faithful life-saving blood transfusions; and some fundamentalists, particularly in the United States, quote Leviticus to justify their belief that homosexuals should be killed.

The Bible is, and always has been, a mixed blessing. Its misuse has caused as much suffering as its proper use has been a blessing. Not only that, there are holy women and men from other religious traditions (and none) who lead spiritual lives without ever seeing a Bible. We may feel reluctant to do it, but leaving our Bible at home won't necessarily impede our spiritual journey; in fact the opposite may be true.

At the end of 'Hello wall' I said that prayer isn't an optional extra, but central to the spiritual endeavour. So am I contradicting myself when I say that nothing in our religion is indispensable to the spiritual life? Well, yes and no. Yes, because prayer as a way of being and becoming is essential; but no, if we imagine that any particular type or style of prayer overrides others.

Not long after I was first ordained I had a chat with a bishop, a caring and loving man, and certainly a man of prayer in both senses of the word. As some readers may know, clergy in the Church of England are required by Cannon Law to say morning and evening prayers every day, and not only say them but lift them from either the Book of Common Prayer (1662) or some other authorised text.

Saying the offices (as morning and evening prayers are known) by myself is something that I have never found in the least bit prayerful. I think I would just as soon read the side of a cornflakes packet. We discussed my concerns and the possible alternative forms of prayer that could be used; he was quite open to my praying in different ways, as long as I said the office first. He said, 'If you're quick, you can get through it in 10 minutes.' Even then, as a relatively young man and newly ordained, I felt that this was simply turning prayer into ritual; it seemed to be much more connected to the strictures of the Pharisees than to the teachings of Jesus.

If prayer in any particular form isn't helping our spiritual growth, not only *can* it be let go, but it *should* be let go. Different traditions within the Christian Church have their own forms of prayer. There's the 'I just want to tell you Lord...' approach of spontaneous prayer within the Evangelical tradition, the 'hands in the air' of the charismatic tradition, or the silent devotions before the crucifix of the Catholic tradition, and many others besides. What becomes destructive of prayer and the spiritual path is an insistence that one particular form is the only right and proper way to pray. All forms *can* be used as expressions of prayer, but none *have* to be.

Having said that no aspect of religion is indispensable to our spiritual life, let me qualify that. There is nothing that is universally indispensable. That is, nothing I take from my religious tradition, nothing that I myself find essential, will necessarily be essential to any other person. It's extremely important to grasp this fact, for two particular reasons.

First, once we recognise that whatever it is that we personally find necessary in our spiritual life is indeed just that – personal – then we're unlikely to take a narrow and dogmatic view of anyone else's spiritual journey. It is the idea that somehow our way is best, or even the only way, that leads to intolerance and bigotry. Once we grasp that our own form of expression isn't in itself crucial, but only helpful, then we're able to accept other people's freedom to choose for themselves as well, without feeling that our own choices are in any way threatened. That's when we can learn from one another because, if nothing is actually imperative, then nothing needs to be fought over or protected.

Second, the realisation that nothing in our religion is actually essential to a spiritual life is immensely liberating. For many people religion is not an enabling asset, but a burden they carry around. It does nothing for them, and they actually feel guilty about that. Some give it up, but others just plod on under the impression that, like foul-tasting medicine, it must somehow be doing them good. And when religion also feels like an ill-fitting garment it restricts our every movement and we die a little every day. To realise that religion itself isn't necessary can, for some people, feel like being let out of prison. Jesus said:

> 'He has sent me to proclaim release to the captives and recovery of sight to the blind, to let the oppressed go free, to proclaim the year of the Lord's favour.' (Luke 4:18-19)

Jesus, the man who sat lightly on religious practice, proclaimed that 'the Sabbath was made for man, not man for the Sabbath'. He overturned many of the laws and customs of his day, putting the needs of the individual above ritualistic practice. Jesus was supremely indifferent to religion; not that he didn't care about it, just that he wasn't attached to it, which is the great secret of healthy religious belief.

Although no ritual or routine is actually necessary, as I have said, we may choose to make religious practice part of our spiritual life.

Most of us feel the need of aids and reminders in many areas of life, and that's no less true for spirituality. If we ask a religion to help us that's fine, as long as we don't become slavishly attached to it because, as soon as we do, it ceases to be an aid and starts to become an anchor. If we maintain a healthy detachment from our religion, we can focus on becoming spiritually alive.

On more than one occasion when people have talked to me about their spiritual life I have suggested that they stop doing something that has been central to lives. It may be to stop reading the Bible for a period, or stop praying in a particular way. The initial response is always one of slight bemusement, but it has, without fail, enabled that person to move on from their stalled position to one of revived spiritual growth. We cling to our habits and beliefs as if they were a life-line, yet so often they turn out to be the cords that bind us.

My wife who also works in mime and physical theatre (a woman of many parts), described to me a performance by a famous French company she had seen. A man entered the stage holding a briefcase. He was attached at the back by ropes that restricted his movements. On the far side of the stage, hanging on a piece of string, was a pair of scissors. The man laboured to get across the stage; several times he almost reached the scissors but was pulled back just before he got there. Everybody in the audience was willing him to reach the scissors. If only he could get there he could cut himself free. Eventually, triumphantly, he reached the scissors, snipped them free from the string that held them. At last he could release himself! Instead, he opened his briefcase to reveal a collection of scissors, added the new pair, and was then dragged offstage by the ropes.

Religion used well frees us to be ourselves and enables us to live a life of love and care with those around us. Religious practice, when we're too attached to it, alienates us from our fellow travellers, narrows our vision and stops us living the sort of liberated existence that is our right and duty as human beings. It's interesting to observe that some modern day atheists are as attached to their doctrines as many religious fanatics of the past were to theirs. Sit lightly on your religion or your atheism – the world will keep spinning without either!

Nothing in my religion is necessary, nothing in your religion is necessary. What we choose to practise, we choose to practise because we want to, but whatever it is we had better do some serious thinking about our motivation. Is it fear, habit or indoctrination? Or does our practice truly enable us to become genuinely spiritual and better human beings?

Be religious by all means, but be so because you want to, be so because it's helpful, and be so in the knowledge that no other living soul has to or ought to be religious in the same way as you.

# CHAPTER 13

## There's nowt so queer as folk

That lovely old Yorkshire (most probably) saying that 'All t'world's queer 'cept thee and me, and I'm not so sure about thee' catches nicely the way we often feel about other people. Why can't they see things the way I do? Well, partly it's to do with psychological type, groupings that help to explain why and how people differ from each other. And that's why I'm dragging psychology into a book on secular spirituality.

In any grouping, it soon becomes obvious that there are basic differences in the way individuals approach life: for example, the laid-back types who let the world roll by; the control freaks who need to organise everything down to the last detail; the hail-fellow-well-met types who are the life and soul of every gathering; and the reserved types who say little and have to be drawn into every conversation.

Differences in the way people see the world and interact with it can either, at one extreme, have a positive effect on a relationship or situation or, on the other, potentially be destructive. Our spiritual journey should be about living life to the full in ourselves, and enabling others to do the same. An understanding of our and other people's psychological types can be one of our many aids on this journey. It helps us to make sense of our reactions in most circumstances, and to understand where others are coming from.

The Swiss psychiatrist and psychotherapist Carl Jung made a study of different types of people, and the way each interacted with the world at large and those around them. This work was advanced by Isabel Myers who, with her mother, Katharine Briggs, developed a psychological 'test' (not really the best label, because preference rather than ability is measured), indicating a person's preferences on a 16-point scale. I won't be going into it in any depth here because that would need a book in itself, but I do think it's worthwhile briefly outlining psychological type because it's so crucial to the way we relate to those around us.

In the first chapter of this book I recounted how I dismally failed to identify the right person in a video of a street crime. Part of this failure I put down to my not being a 'sensing' person. Until I went on a Myers-Briggs Type Indicator (MBTI) weekend, I really had little appreciation that different types of people really do perceive the world in very different ways, yet this clearly is the case. It's helpful to know and understand this type difference when encountering somebody who just cannot 'see' what I 'see', or when I cannot 'see' what they 'see'. Here's an example.

My wife and I had been married for a number of years before we both, at different times, went on an MBTI weekend. In all of those previous years, our holidays were always a little contentious. I like to relax with a pile of books (which I may or may not read) and do very little. For me, holiday is about space to do nothing. Ruth, on the other hand, likes to be up and doing. Sports, walks, exploration, visiting; for her, holiday is about recharging her batteries by engaging in activity with a lot of external stimulus. Holidays always ended up as a compromise that neither of us found very satisfying. Either I would be worn-out by too much activity, or Ruth would be bored.

Ring any bells? Holidays are often a family nightmare, rather than a time of refreshment and enjoyment. Why? Because different psychological types are refreshed in different ways. Ruth's ideal is my nightmare, and vice-versa. Having both completed an MBTI weekend, we found that of the four scales, we differed on one, the introvert-extravert scale.

Carl Jung introduced the terms introvert and extravert to our language and they're now used to indicate that someone is either shy and retiring (introvert), or boisterous and gregarious (extravert – in common parlance now usually spelled 'extrovert'). Often the former is thought of in negative terms, while the latter attracts more positive connotations. In fact, in Jung's original definition, neither is better or worse. In fact, no value judgement is attached to any of the 16 types developed in the MBTI. Our psychological ID can be likened to whether we are left- or right-handed. At a push, we can use either hand, but we prefer one over the other.

To be introverted means preferring to spend your energies on internal rather than external matters; ideas and concepts are more important than activity. Introverts are more likely to want to think everything through before uttering a word, and are usually quite happy with their own company, or in the company of just a few people well known to them. They prefer their own space and a certain amount of peace and quiet. If that isn't available, introverts are likely to become worn out and function less ably. To recharge their batteries, introverts will usually need a certain degree of quiet and space so they're not overtaxed by too much external demand or stimulus.

Extraverts, though, prefer to expend their energies on the external world. Action and interaction are vital if the extravert is to function properly. Thinking is often done out loud in a constant stream, as ideas are bounced off others and thought processes are developed. Extraverts will usually enjoy the company of lots of people (but not always), and breadth of social contact will be favoured over depth. To recharge their batteries, extraverts will want to interact with the environment in an active way. External stimulus is the very stuff of their lives.

Knowing this about ourselves didn't instantly cure the holiday mismatch for Ruth and me, but at least we then appreciated each other's needs and could build that into the two-week programme. We now give ourselves space and permission to do our own thing without feeling that our relationship is flawed in some way. Knowing about psychological type doesn't change the reality, but understanding it does stop differences from becoming disasters.

Earlier I mentioned my sensing weakness. The second part of the MBTI scale checks how we prefer to perceive the world. Having already noted in Chapter 1 that perception is a creative process, what this scale does is highlight the way our creative processes prefer to function. The perceptive scale divides us into those who are predominantly sensing and those who are intuitive. Those are two ways of 'seeing', both equally valid, but each very different from the other.

The person who favours the sensing perceptive process is very much set in the here and now. They use their five senses to make sense (literally) of their surroundings and will interpret reality according to what is actually in their immediate environment. The sensing person has a good eye for detail, and will probably be able to recall a scene with far greater literal accuracy than an intuitive person. A sensing person is grounded in the present and good at interpreting the facts as they are, but won't tend to be as good at seeing other possibilities.

The intuitive person will tend to be less able to absorb concrete reality, sometimes missing what is at the end of their nose. The intuitive person's strength lies in seeing possibilities and implications. They concentrate not on what is in the present, but in the future, on where things may lead, or what the probable outcome might be. Intuitives tend to be good ideas people, creative and imaginative, but might not be so good at actually getting things done.

Some time ago, while I was driving up the motorway to Oxford, my mind was way ahead of the here and now. Where will I park? How many roundabouts do I need to negotiate? Will I arrive on time? I was using my preferred intuition function, allowing my sensing function to take a back seat. As a result I completely failed to see the exit sign for Oxford, huge as it was, so missed my turn-off. A very long detour meant that I arrived only just in time.

It's easy when working or living with someone who perceives the world differently from us, to feel they're just being awkward. The sensing person might think 'Why on earth can't she just stick to the facts', while the intuitive person would be thinking 'Can't he see what will happen if we do it his way?' It can be a recipe for disaster and discord, argument and truculence. Yet it needn't be so. Each function is as vital as another.

When people of different perceptual orientations understand psychological type, they see their opposite number not as a threat but as someone who will complement and assist the process in which they're involved. It could be in a marriage, or at work, in school (a child who perceives things differently from her or his teacher might be in serious trouble if the teacher isn't aware of type difference), or in our leisure activities. Committee meetings (PTA, scouts, church, residents' association, bowling club... you name it) are usually fraught with people at odds with one another. When we begin to grasp the implication of psychological type differences, the likelihood of constructive dialogue and increased co-operation becomes enormous.

The third category in the MBTI scale concerns the way we judge or organise the world – the way that we come to conclusions. Having perceived the world in a particular way, we then handle that information in two quite different ways. The MBTI calls them thinking and feeling. As with the categories above, we all have and use both functions, we simply prefer one to the other. To be a thinker doesn't mean you have no feelings, nor does it mean that feeling people cannot use their brains. Those whose preferred way of organising the world is thinking, tend to be logical and cool-headed in their approach. They will consider all the facts and 'balance the books' in accord with practical and rational principles. The strength of the thinking type is making analytical and matter-of-fact decisions consistent with clear-cut criteria. The weakness is a tendency to overlook the human element, and that can have serious consequences. Bad industrial relations are almost certain to follow decisions made by a solely 'thinking' management team.

Those who prefer to organise or judge their world through feelings do so keeping the human element in the forefront of their minds. Decisions will be based on how they affect people. Will they like it? Can they do it? Is it pleasing? The strength of this approach is that you're likely to carry people with you because you're being sensitive to their needs; the weakness is that the basic facts may be ignored. A management team made up of all 'feelers' would probably have the work force with them – right up to the point when the company goes bust.

Again, a good team will be a balance of people of both preferences who will value one another for the insights they both bring to decisions. I heard a story of a hospital that needed to close some of its wards. One plan was to close a maternity ward and combine it with a gynaecological ward. On paper this seemed to make sense. All the evidence of location, specialisation, equipment usage etc pointed to it being the perfect solution. My guess is that all those involved in that decision were 'thinkers'. The facts pointed to it, so the conclusion was obvious. Had there been a fair representation of 'feelers' on the committee, they would probably have pointed out the inhumanity of placing women who had miscarried or had needed an abortion next to those with healthy babies or, perhaps even more painfully, next to a woman who had suffered a still-birth. Thinking and feeling need each other to ensure a balanced and truly spiritual lifestyle.

The three sets of categories above are those worked on by Jung. Myers added a fourth that indicates which of the perceiving options (sensing/intuition) and of the judging options (thinking/feeling) is displayed most fully to the outside world. If a person is strongest on perception, rather than judging, and his preference is sensing, then that is the element of his psychological type that will be most evident to those around him. If, on the other hand, a person is stronger on judging, and his or her preference is feeling, then feeling is what those nearby will be most aware of.

At the end of an MBTI workshop you are presented with a set of letters representing your most likely preferred psychological type. The four polarity scales are:

| | | |
|---|---|---|
| 1 | Extravert (E) | Introvert (I) |
| 2 | Sensing (S) | Intuitive (N) |
| 3 | Thinking (T) | Feeling (F) |
| 4 | Judging (J) | Perceiving (P) |

From the four scales the possibility of 16 combinations emerges. The preferences each psychological type are briefly summarised in a written report which also assesses how they interact with the world. When I first read mine, it was like reading my autobiography.

Part of the spiritual journey, as I have outlined above, is getting to know ourselves. The MBTI is a useful indicator of psychological type and can help us become more aware of who we are – with all our strengths and weaknesses, needs and skills. Our psychological type colours all that we are and do. I am an INFP. Perhaps you will recognise my type in the biases that are undoubtedly present in this book.

In one short chapter I can do no more than scrape the surface of psychological type. For those who hope to live a spiritual life, a life of positive interaction with others, it is important that they at least acknowledge the concept of psychological type, even if they don't wish to go into further detail. Much of who we are and, consequently, the decisions we make, are affected by our own type and by the type of those with whom we have to deal in life. A spiritual life is a life lived to the full, to its greatest potential; knowledge of what makes us and others tick can greatly enhance the process. A little knowledge may be a dangerous thing, but no knowledge at all can be disastrous.

# PART TWO

# CHAPTER 14

## Do you feel myth-understood?

Myth-understood? No, that isn't my dyslexia playing up. Being myth-understood happens to me quite a lot. In our rational and scientific age, where truth is thought to be objective, factual, historic and concrete, we have lost the ability to recognise truth in its less tangible forms. At least, that seems to be the case in some areas of life.

In Chapter 10 I quoted the Rabbie Burns line, 'My love is like a red, red rose' to emphasise that that simile is still very much part of our language. It's a line that resonates in the heart of anyone who has been in love. To argue literally that it isn't true, that my love doesn't have a prickly stem and petals, wouldn't enter most people's heads. In matters of the heart, especially where erotic love is concerned, analogy and poetry make complete sense.

Once we move away from that realm of experience, however, something seems to click in people's brains and the 21st-century rationalist takes over. Yet as I have argued already, the most important area of our lives, that which gives *meaning* to life, lies not in the observable realm, but in cojective experience. The sense of meaninglessness that haunts so many people, can be pinned on the fact that they're not in a relationship – not with themselves, not with others, not with their environment.

When a cojective interrelation is missing, people feel like objects, devoid of personal worth. Their behaviour patterns reflect this belief either in anti-social action, and/or neurotic or psychotic symptoms. In debunking the job lot of religion, superstition, lores and fables, our modern scientific age has thrown out the baby with the bath water. In bygone ages many myths were thought to be literally true, but with advances in scientific knowledge such interpretations are now quite sensibly dismissed. But to discard the story entirely is perhaps even more foolish.

It isn't that we don't enjoy a good story these days – we certainly do. Despite the appeal of television and DVDs, a good film still attracts large cinema audiences, and the reason some films are so successful is that they touch a point of human consciousness that's alive to the cojective. The hit *Star Wars* trilogy was not only technically brilliant in its day, but it exploited myths about our humanity: the struggle between our dark side and our spiritual side (I'm not so sure about the later prequels). Harry Potter's success, in book and film, and the huge acclaim accorded *The Lord of the Rings* film trilogy, underline our love of a good story. Classics such as *The Lion, the Witch and the Wardrobe*, beloved by children for decades, have also been brought wonderfully to life in the cinema for new generations.

The great difference between the present and past ages is not that we no longer enjoy a good story, but that we dismiss it as just that – a good story and nothing more. Before the 18th-century Enlightenment, when rational and scientific knowledge asserted themselves, people thought the Bible myths were literally true. As the accumulation of knowledge proved that wasn't the case, the power of such stories faded because they didn't accord with the evidence. And from then until now the Church has been fighting a rearguard action, slowly conceding that some of the Bible's more colourful tales aren't literally true after all.

First we had the creation stories in Genesis. It had been considered heresy to question the categorical truth of the Garden of Eden story. Of course a snake conversed with Eve, tempting her with an apple – it was the word of God! Now, the proportion of Christians who believe in the literalness of this story is small. Yesterday's heresy becomes today's orthodoxy. But the Church is slow to adapt and revise its thinking. I was interested to read that it took the Roman Catholic Church more than 350 years to admit, officially, that it had been wrong to brand Galileo a heretic for claiming that the earth was not the centre of the universe. Even then it took a Vatican enquiry several years to come to that conclusion.

Within the Church these days, however, the pendulum has swung to such an extent that there now seems a general reluctance to take myth seriously at all. Truth for the majority of people, including most Christians, has come to mean that which is objectively and literally true. The word 'myth' is defined by most of us as 'a story that isn't true'.

When, in 1977, a group of theologians published a book called *The Myth of God Incarnate*, all hell broke loose. Many people, some of whom I suspect had never read the book, basically accused the authors of saying that the Jesus story itself wasn't true. This stubborn insistence that truth can only be found in literal and objective interpretation is not only blinkered and naive, as history has demonstrated only too frequently, but it denies the most fundamentally important aspect of humanity, namely that meaning lies in the cojective relationship, and not in objective criteria.

A story that is also a myth may or may not be literally accurate, and may or may not have actually happened at some point in history. But it's vital to grasp that neither point is important in itself. In fact it may be more important to accept that a myth is not literally true in order to understand it properly. What, after all, does 'My love is like a red, red rose' mean if taken literally? It's a nonsense. Likewise, many biblical stories taken at face value simply look embarrassing. Let's try an old favourite:

> 'So they picked Jonah up and threw him into the sea;
> and the sea ceased from its raging. Then the men feared
> the Lord even more, and they offered a sacrifice to the
> Lord and made vows. But the Lord provided a large
> fish to swallow up Jonah; and Jonah was in the belly of
> the fish three days and three nights.' (Jonah 1:15-17)

If I had a pound for every time that I've heard the literal truth of this story debated, I would be a wealthy man. Because people get stuck on this one detail the whole point of the story is missed. Historically, there never was a man called Jonah, at least not this particular Jonah. The story was written by an unknown author at a time when the people of Israel were being particularly exclusive in their attitudes. They believed they were the only people God cared about; everyone else was 'beyond the pale'. The point of the story has nothing to do with the 'big fish', but rather is contained at the end where God shows mercy to Nineveh. This myth or parable was written for no other reason than to show readers that God's love was greater than their exclusive behaviour. To get caught up in whether or not it actually happened at a time and place in history, is like trying to identify the spot on the road where the Good Samaritan rescued the beleaguered traveller. Repeat after me:

> Myth is a story that conveys a spiritual truth – it is a story about you and me; not to be believed in, but to be lived out. It is a story about something that never was, but always is.

Myth is concerned with cojective experience, with what gives meaning to life; it is concerned with our relationships and what makes life worth living. Myth is true, not because something actually happened, but because it encapsulates the truth of what it means to be a human being, with all our hopes and fears, joys and sorrows, successes and failures. In many ways myth is *truer* than concrete fact. Myth is concerned with what it means to know and be known as a person; objective fact is to do with knowing about and being known about; the difference is one of quality.

Many people today, in increasing numbers, are giving up on religion. I'm not surprised. Not only can the liturgy (formal worship) be tedious and long-winded, but the words of the service, and the sermons, give the impression that to be a Christian means to believe in fairy tales. Children are often part of the Church until they start to think critically. That's when a whole package of nonsense gets thrown out. When Father Christmas and fairies get the big heave-ho, so do the virgin birth and angels; they're seen in much the same light and to have about the same relevance in a technological age.

That's a pity. The myths of the Christian tradition, like the myths of the other great religions, hold within them eternal truths. We don't have to jettison the whole package, we simply have to understand the nature of the beast we're dealing with. In its inadequate way, religion is a storehouse of treasures; its myths speak to us, not of some supernatural other world, or past events, nor of some objective moral standard to which we must conform. The myths of religion speak of the spiritual life, of a quality of being which is about personal relationships, and about who we have it within us to be.

It is not my intention to try to persuade people back into religion. Institutionalised religion is not for everyone even at its best, and at its worst it is positively death-dealing to the spiritual life. What I want to emphasise is this: although the Church and other religions have often failed in the past, and continue to fail today, nevertheless the spiritual truths that lie at their heart and are contained in their myths, are of constant and universal relevance. Myth is your story and my story, and when we enter into it, we are able to live a quality of life that's eternal. Like love and art and beauty, myth has to be understood cojectively not objectively; to reject myth is to deny ourselves a source of wisdom that is enabling for the spiritual traveller.

To my fellow Christians who insist that the Bible, or the New Testament in particular, must be accepted as literal and historical truth, I want to say this: I do not wish to convert you. If your belief enables you to live a life that is full and free and liberating, that's fine. But, please, do not insist that your reality is the only reality; it may be for you, but it is not for me, nor is it for millions of others.

Please reflect on history. The Church has tortured and killed in support of so called 'objective beliefs', subsequently proven wrong. Please understand – myth is not a denial of the truth, it is the highest form of truth, a truth that objective facts alone can never encompass.

In the following chapters I will be treating the Gospels, Matthew, Mark, Luke and John as myth. In doing so I will not be denying the life and the reality of Jesus, nor that he was put to death by crucifixion. Those events are as factual as anything else in ancient history. Nor am I denying that many reported incidents actually happened. Myth does not necessarily deny historicity; what it does do is assert that regardless of how much of the Gospels is verifiable history, there is a truth there that trumps objective fact. It is a universal truth about the nature of humanity that transcends the limited and particular events of history.

# CHAPTER 15

## Old book – new look

As I have suggested, the Bible stories shouldn't be interpreted in literal historical terms alone. The real significance of scripture (of whatever religion) is that the relevance of the story remains true for every generation. For the first seventeen hundred years since the time of Jesus, the educated world view remained much the same: earth was the centre of the universe, heaven was located above the dome of the sky where God lived and, below earth, hell waited. And although during the 18th and 19th centuries this view came to be increasingly questioned, it wasn't really until the 20th century, when scientific knowledge accelerated at astonishing speed, that the world view of the Bible no longer connected with people's understanding of life and the universe.

Increasingly science 'disproved' the Bible; the first cosmonaut proclaimed, having 'been there', that there was no God in heaven – a triumph for an atheist state. Today's generation, at least in technologically advanced countries, is so far removed from the 1st-century Middle East's understanding of the universe that connections can no longer be made. Yet there's still an unbroken strand stretching between the two, and that strand is basic human nature itself. One only needs to read the history and literature of then and now to realise that, although perceptions change as knowledge expands and differing cultures influence one another, women and men remain, at heart, the same.

While I am highly critical of religion, especially its institutionalised forms, nevertheless there remains at its core a wisdom, an essential truth, that is ageless because it expresses the fundamental realities of what it means to be human. Many believe that Jesus, the man, is someone they can relate to, yet the doctrines and creeds that have accreted around him over the centuries have turned him into a figure of disbelief. Every Sunday millions of Christians stand up in church and recite the creed, yet I know for a fact that many simply do not believe, at least literally, in what they're saying – and that is true both for laity and clergy alike. There's an appalling lack of integrity in the Church; it uses language and doctrinal formulations of bygone times and refuses to accept that we now live in a very different world. Its insistence on 'orthodox' belief forces many to be untrue to themselves or simply to vote with their feet and abandon the Church altogether. Or not join it in the first place.

Not surprisingly huge numbers of people are heading in the latter direction. An institution that proclaims ownership of the ultimate truth, so forcing many of its members to live a lie will, of course, lose all credibility in the end. Yet it need not; as an institution the Church needs only to recognise that it is intellectually legitimate to hold more than one view on the same subject. Surely what people believe matters less than how it affects their day-to-day life – how they walk the walk. When I read the Gospels, the picture of Jesus I get isn't one of a man who's overly fussed about other people's beliefs, but rather about how they live their lives. Issues of love, compassion, justice and mercy seem to dominate his teaching and life, not matters of belief.

The Church has perhaps been on the wrong track since earliest times, or at least is getting its priorities wrong. Once the first-hand experience of Jesus and the apostles was lost, then secondhand belief set in like a series of Chinese whispers. Jesus was concerned with right living and right relationships (orthopraxis); the Church as an institution has been concerned with right beliefs *about* Jesus (orthodoxy). The switch was from first-hand living to secondhand living – ie, from spirituality to religion.

The four Gospels were written not as biographies or historical documents, but as proclamations of faith. To assist a fresh understanding of the Gospels for our generation, I want to reach past the religious life of the Church and seek the spiritual experience of Jesus himself. This I propose to do by interpreting some of the 'life events' of Jesus in the light of modern psychological understanding.

Note the inverted commas around 'life events'. That's because I have no wish to debate whether or not some of them actually happened or the form they took; what these stories represent is of far greater importance. We're dealing with myth, remember, and myth is a story in which we're invited to involve ourselves and make our own. These stories are significant not because they're unique or uniquely powerful – the recollections of a superhuman interloper – but because they represent you and me; they are archetypes of the human condition.

Traditionally the life of Jesus, his teaching, death and resurrection are understood as acts of salvation. The sins of humanity, starting with Adam's 'original sin' – his love of apples – through every sin committed ever since, are supposed to have been expunged by Jesus's death on the cross. However, the fact that Jesus descended from heaven precisely in order to be killed and so 'pay the price of sin', seems to me a thoroughly good reason for not believing in God.

The idea that any being requires a blood sacrifice to be made as recompense for being wronged is revolting enough, but to suggest that an all-powerful being requires such an act is literally beyond belief. Yet it has been part of the belief structure of many primitive cultures. Blood sacrifice, human or animal, was thought necessary to placate the relevant deity. Animal sacrifice was part of Jewish ritual at the time of Jesus, so it's no wonder that his death was interpreted in this way. But we have moved on since then. We have indoor plumbing now, television, mobile phones, aeroplanes, nuclear warheads and space travel. Our world is nothing like that of 1st-century Palestine, so why on earth should our beliefs remain unchanged?

The life of Jesus was interpreted *by* people of his time *for* people of his time, but what may have been good enough for St Paul emphatically isn't good enough for us. If the life of Jesus is to mean anything at all to those of us living in the first half of the 21st century with our sophisticated technological toys, then it must be spelled out in language we recognise. To revivify Jesus for contemporary society we need not strip away the myth, for myth is the medium through which truth is conveyed, but rather create new myths for a new age. Jesus himself said it, yet the Church seems hell-bent on ignoring it:

> 'No one sews a piece of un-shrunk cloth on an old cloak, for the patch pulls away from the cloak, and a

worse tear is made. Neither is new wine put into old
wineskins; otherwise, the skins burst, and the wine
is spilled, and the skins are destroyed; new wine is
put into fresh wineskins, and so both are preserved.'
(Matthew 9:16-17)

Jesus's teaching and his entire mode of living demands a new
response from every age. To continue trying to understand him in
the light of 1st-century theology is indeed to put new wine into old
wineskins; as a consequence both are ruined and the message of one of
the world's great human thinkers becomes distorted and 'undrinkable'.
The 'new wineskins' of psychology is a way of expressing in modern
terms the eternal truths lived out and taught by Jesus.

What I'll be suggesting in the following pages won't appeal to
everyone. Nor is it meant to. What I'm most concerned about is, first,
that the wisdom and truth embodied in the person of Jesus isn't lost
on a modern age because the packaging is archaic; second, that there
is an intellectually honest way to affirm the life of Jesus and all that he
stood for, without having to compromise one's integrity by pretending
to subscribe to beliefs that are untenable in this day and age.

In the following chapters we'll be looking at five 'events' in the
life of Jesus: Birth and Beginnings, Wilderness, Transfiguration,
Death, and resurrection and Ascension. By addressing these 'events'
psychologically it is possible to reintroduce them to our own time and
our own spiritual journey. That is not to suggest we should attempt to
emulate Jesus, which has been one of the Church's biggest mistakes.
We're not meant to be like Christ, but rather Christ-like. This is not to
bandy words frivolously, but to make a crucial distinction. To try to be
like Christ is to try to copy him, which is to live a secondhand life. To
be Christ-like, however, is to be like him inasmuch as he was fully and
authentically himself. This is what Jesus's message is all about: living a
valid life, being ourselves and, in so doing, relating to others in a fully
meaningful way.

By seeing Jesus in this way, as an exemplar for our own complete
humanity, Christianity comes alive in a way it never can when Jesus
is conceived of as being of a different order from the rest of us. As the
Son of God he becomes a figure bigger than history, to be believed in
or not, as the case may be, but, as a human being who lived his life to

the full, as a person who gives us a sense of what we have it in us to become, he challenges us to live life like that too.

Here we reach the heart of what it means to be a spiritual person. It isn't about believing certain things, or emulating someone else's life, no matter how worthy. Nor is it about being conventionally religious. Rather, and quite simply, it's about living one's life authentically; to be fully and truly who we are, no more and no less. And Jesus is our model, enabling us to enter into that quality of living we call divine, known in the Gospels as the Kingdom of Heaven. It is life lived with the quality of eternity.

A saint who lived in the 2nd century, Irenaeus, summed up in a few words the nature of spirituality thus: 'The glory of God is a human being who is fully alive.'

However we conceive of God, or indeed whether we conceive of God existing at all in conventional theistic terms, doesn't really matter. A human being who is fully alive should be the aim of our spiritual journey. If contemplating the life of Jesus from a psychological perspective strengthens this goal for you, then fine; if it doesn't, then forget it. The vital thing is that we enter into the myth so that it transforms us and helps us embrace our own potential. Each person will need to do this in her or his own way, finding the truth that will resonate with their own inner truth. The poet Robert Browning in *Paracelsus* expresses it nicely:

> *...There is an inmost centre in us all,*
> *Where truth abides in fullness; and around,*
> *Wall upon wall, the gross flesh hems it in,*
> *This perfect clear perception – which is truth*
> *...and to KNOW,*
> *Rather consists in opening out a way*
> *Whence the imprisoned splendour may escape,*
> *Than in effecting entry for a light*
> *Supposed to be without.*

The language of psychology is one way through which modern humanity can once again engage with myth and find ancient truths resonating in contemporary ideas. To allow this to happen is to have one's perception changed, to be 'born again', which takes us on to the first life event of Jesus... his birth.

# CHAPTER 16

## Birth and beginnings

The first event, of course, is the birth of Jesus. Two of the four Gospels recount the nativity story – virgin birth, angels, shepherds, wise men and so forth – the other two don't mention it. For me that is significant – solid evidence that we're dealing not with history, but with story. If facts such as a virgin birth were known to be historically sound, one would expect it to have been an essential part of the message from the beginning. As it is, only half the Gospels record it and it is conspicuously absent from the letters of St Paul, the earliest writings of the Church.

Yet stories of the virgin birth should not be dismissed out of hand; along with other material they point to an important psychological truth – that our birth is not simply a once only physical experience, but a continuing psychological process. In the prologue to the fourth Gospel, St John (1:12-13) writes:

'But to all who received him, who believed in his name, he gave power to become children of God, who were born, not of blood or of the will of the flesh or of the will of man, but of God.'

Being born 'not of blood or of the will of the flesh or of the will of man, but of God' sounds very much like a descriptive variation on virgin birth. But the writer isn't talking about the birth of Jesus here, but of every Christian believer. The spiritual truth embedded in the nativity stories is made even more explicit by John: Jesus's virgin birth is a model for our own spiritual birth, and it is a theme that is explored throughout the Gospels.

In a very real sense each of us has two births. We emerge physically, but we are spiritual and psychological beings as well. Our progress to physical maturity is, on the whole, a steady one over the first 20 years or so. Our psychological and spiritual growth is far less certain, however, and depends largely upon our interactions with others.

Psychological birth is a process rather than an event, one we can be increasingly open to, or one we can choose to close off and shut down. To speak of a virgin birth is to speak spiritually or psychologically, not literally and physically. Someone 'born of a virgin' is a woman or man who is spiritually and psychologically open and alive. It is easy to forget, reading the Gospels as we do, that the life and teaching of Jesus came first; the stories *about* Jesus came later, and a good many years later at that. Jesus's teaching had a lot to say about being psychologically open but, naturally, he used the language of his day not ours. He spoke of being 'born again', and of the need to become like little children. Those are profound insights into psychological and spiritual well-being and, as such, are as true today as they were when he first uttered them.

When our daughter, Freya, was quite small and just beginning to learn a basic vocabulary, she made the sort of mistake every child does at that stage. Living near to the Thames, we'd quite often go down and feed the ducks. At first everything that splashed around and ate the bread was 'duck'. After a while she began to discriminate between ducks, coots, geese etc, a process the Swiss psychologist Jean Piaget labelled assimilation and accommodation. At first, Freya had a very basic frame of reference, and all animals with wings that swam and ate bread were 'duck'. Any new breed that happened along was assimilated into her 'duck' category. Put simply, assimilation is a process by which we bend the facts to fit what we already know. As children grow and their experience and knowledge expands, so they learn to accommodate. In learning to distinguish between ducks, coots and geese, Freya altered her own frame of reference to accommodate external facts rather than 'bending' them.

This process, of course, continues throughout childhood. In a sense it marks a constant preparedness to be proved wrong, then learn something new and move on. Although children can seem stubborn in the face of facts they cannot accommodate, it isn't true stubbornness, but frustration at being presented with awkward facts that force a rethink. Once children have reached the stage where comprehension comes easily, they are only too willing to accommodate. In short, psychologically speaking, children live through a process of constant rebirth. Every time they release a wrongly assimilated piece of information and accommodate their thinking to a more exact reality, they have, in a small way, been 'born again'.

> 'At that time the disciples came to Jesus and asked, "Who is the greatest in the kingdom of heaven?" He called a child, whom he put among them, and said, "Truly I tell you, unless you change and become like children, you will never enter the kingdom of heaven. Whoever becomes humble like this child is the greatest in the kingdom of heaven."' (Matthew 18:1-4)

All too often, this saying of Jesus has been interpreted as meaning that we'll only get to heaven (after death) if we're dependent, meek and subservient in this life. Nothing could be further from what I believe Jesus meant by this. First off, the kingdom of heaven is a metaphor for the quality of life we ought to be abiding by now, not post mortem. But more important, it has nothing to do with being meek and submissive and suppressing our willingness to think for ourselves (which is how the Church often treats its members). Instead it has everything to do with being willing to process information for ourselves. Who is greatest in the kingdom of heaven? She or he who is willing to keep a thoughtful but open mind – prejudice is not on the agenda.

There are two critical words in the passage above, from Matthew: 'change' and 'humble'. To change is to make a conscious decision to be different. In this context it is deciding not to prejudge any situation from a position of incomplete knowledge. How hard that is! It means not falling back on comfortable stereotypes, but assessing new situations and people from scratch 'with the eyes of a child'. By so doing, Jesus himself could challenge many of the norms and assumptions of his own time. He was alive to the moment, not shackled to the past, and could see what others could not because he was open to possibilities not probabilities. The humility of the child comes from her or his freedom from vanity. That may sound obvious, but all too often it's the obvious that's easiest to miss.

So what is the substance of such vanity? Surely the feeling that we've made it, that we have the answers, the power, the wealth, the feeling that in any given area of life we have arrived. The humility of the child is sourced to quite the opposite state of mind, to knowing that it has far to go, and has much to learn. Change is possible only if we feel the need or desire to improve; humility is knowledge that change is not only desirable, but essential if we're to enjoy full psychological health.

As John Henry Newman put it: 'Here below, to live is to change, and to be perfect is to have changed often.' Failure to change and adapt, willingly or otherwise, indicates that we've fallen short on our ability to accommodate. Instead, new facts, new situations are assimilated, shoehorned into preconceived notions and judged by old criteria that may be totally irrelevant, inappropriate or inaccurate. Such people, with such mental rigidity, cause distress to themselves and to those they live and work with. Every living thing changes constantly, and not to do so is to die. That is true psychologically and spiritually as well as organically.

In his encounter with Nicodemus, Jesus emphasised what it takes to live his kind of life. Here, Nicodemus talks first about the nature of Jesus's life, after which Jesus tells him what is required of anybody wishing to 'see the kingdom of God':

> 'Now there was a Pharisee named Nicodemus, a leader of the Jews. He came to Jesus by night and said to him, "Rabbi, we know that you are a teacher who has come from God; for no one can do these signs that you do apart from the presence of God." Jesus answered him, "Very truly, I tell you, no one can see the kingdom of God without being born from above." Nicodemus said to him, "How can anyone be born after having grown old? Can he enter a second time into the mother's womb and be born?" Jesus answered, "Very truly, I tell you, no one can enter the kingdom of God without being born of water and spirit. What is born of the flesh is flesh, and what is born of the Spirit is spirit. Do not be astonished that I have said to you, 'You must be born from above.' The wind blows where it

chooses, and you hear the sound of it, but you do not know where it comes from or where it goes. So it is with everyone who is born of the Spirit.'" (John 3:1-8)

From what Jesus is saying it may seem that everyone born of the Spirit is unpredictable; you know neither where they are coming from nor where they are going. That is also true of anyone who is in the habit of accommodating. Such people will adjust their perceptions to suit the circumstances, so cannot be expected to produce identical answers every time. You don't know where they're going because the process of accommodation is a creative one that produces unique reactions. Would that our politicians were less prone to assimilating everything into the Party 'line', and felt more able to accommodate the real needs of the electorate.

It's an unfortunate fact that most adults seem to think that they've done quite enough accommodating by the time they reach their early twenties. Of course, no one stops altogether, but the process becomes drastically reduced, and any new information is assimilated into already formulated templates. The old saying that 'there's none so blind as those that will not see' defines the assimilator. Life becomes limited and narrow, not because external circumstances demand it, but because perceptions atrophy. The robust spiritual life, on the other hand, is lived to the full, embracing psychological maturity which, in turn, calls for a constant attitude of accommodation.

It has been my experience as a counsellor, therapist and spiritual director, that problems occur when people are unable or unwilling to move on, to adjust to new circumstances. The greater the degree of psychological immobility, the greater the distress.

Jesus's teaching about being 'born again' is not asking us to accept a particular religious experience. Too many born-again Christians simply swap one set of values for another and then assimilate everything into that revised template. They remain just as narrow as they've ever been, sometimes more so, everything being hemmed in by a particular religious perception. Being born again in the sense Jesus meant it is, I believe, a conscious decision to change. It is being prepared to return to that childhood state of innocence where everything is provisional and assessed on its merits. The spiritual truth of this teaching is eternal. 'We will never see the kingdom of

God'; that is, we will never live life with an eternal quality unless we accept the need for constant accommodation. The need to be 'born again', or 'born of the Spirit' is crucial to the teaching and life of Jesus.

He knew then what modern counselling and psychotherapy may express differently, but which utter the same underlying truths. People live dysfunctional lives if they become fixed in their responses to life. The degree of dysfunction will depend on the extent to which a person becomes stuck in their emotional responses and/or their thinking. If an individual can find the wherewithal to change – which usually means a change in perception – then she or he may well experience a feeling of being 'born again', almost literally. There's a liberation from patterns of thought and behaviour that restrict and confine.

The therapeutic process of being born again can be experienced in many ways. Religion at its best can do it, psychotherapy and counselling can do it, and so can entering into a loving relationship with a partner who allows you to feel accepted for the person you really are. Being born again, in other words undergoing a 'virgin birth', is a human experience available to us all – an experience that leads to a life lived to the full.

The story of Jesus's virgin birth must not be taken in isolation, but in conjunction with his teaching on being born again and on becoming like little children. Whether or not one wishes to believe that it is historical truth, is of much less importance than the realisation that it is the model for our personal growth into psychological and spiritual wholeness.

# CHAPTER 17

## Wilderness – finding our way

The story of Jesus's sojourn in the wilderness appears in three of the four Gospels. In Mark, generally accepted as the earliest, we hear that:

> '...the Spirit immediately drove him out into the wilderness. He was in the wilderness forty days, tempted by Satan; and he was with the wild beasts; and the angels waited on him.' (Mark 1:12-13)

Matthew and Luke give us more elaborate versions that include specific temptations by the devil. So what are we to make of these stories? Do they speak to us at the beginning of the 21st century? The idea of a devil incarnate and ministering angels cuts little ice, I'd suggest, even among the devout. For those who give little thought to religious symbolism, they represent further evidence that the Christian establishment expects the faithful to believe almost anything.

Yet 'wilderness' is a reality, in literal terms; that is, where people choose to go with the express intention of 'listening to their own inner voice'. It's also a psychological reality that we all experience – often at times of anguish and distress, when we're no longer certain of our direction, our relationships, or whether life has any purpose. Even if life has generally been good to you, you will, so long as you've passed through adolescence, have experienced feelings of wilderness.

In the Bible such themes runs through the text like a thread. In chapter three of Genesis, after Adam and Eve have eaten the forbidden fruit they are cast out of the garden into what sounds very much like a wilderness:

> 'Cursed is the ground because of you; in toil you shall eat of it all the days of your life; thorns and thistles it shall bring forth for you; and you shall eat the plants of the field. By the sweat of your face you shall eat bread until you return to the ground, for out of it you were taken; you are dust, and to dust you shall return.' (Genesis 3:17-19)

Compared with the Garden of Eden, all the world is a wilderness in which we have to work hard to find our place. Mostly the Eden story is regarded as depicting the onset of evil following humanity's disobedience of God. (It is the archetypal buck-passing tale: man blames woman and woman blames serpent. But the real culprit here is God – he expects Eve to know the difference between good and evil before she has eaten the fruit of that particular tree.)

A more positive interpretation of the Genesis myth is to see it as humanity's journey from a state of childhood innocence, through rebellious adolescence to adult maturity. Generally speaking, girls do mature into women earlier than boys into men, so that the idea of Eve leading the way out of childlike innocence into the wilderness of early adulthood is a fair depiction of what actually happens both physically and psychologically.

One cannot speak universally about the experience of adolescence because different cultures have differing traditions and rites of passage. In general terms, though, it can be regarded as that period, somewhere between early teens and mid-twenties, when body chemistry asserts itself, sex matters and questions of identity and belonging intrude themselves. Turmoil, to a greater or lesser extent, replaces the tranquillity of childhood (which isn't to say that our earliest years are necessarily good or happy; external circumstances may well overwhelm any period of innocent calm, but there is less internal conflict at this time). Then adolescence is a time of wilderness, out of which our adult identity emerges.

As King Lear says to his daughter Cordelia, 'nothing will come of nothing'. The young adult we become depends very much on the extent to which we've been able to work successfully through our adolescent difficulties. Our adult identity, therefore, isn't just presented as a gift, out of the blue, but emerges from the complex brew of genetic inheritance, nurture (or lack of it) as infants and children, and interaction with the world we live in.

Being parent to an adolescent is one of the most difficult tasks anyone has to face. Hitting the right balance between being supportive and allowing freedom on the one hand, and challenging destructive behaviour and insisting on boundaries on the other, is an almost impossible line to tread successfully. Sometimes we, as parents or responsible adults, get it wrong; we're over-protective or too liberal, we're either too authoritarian or uncaring, and the struggle of the young adults with whom we share our lives will reawaken in us struggles that were not fully worked through in our own youth.

Becoming an integrated personality not only involves the wilderness period of adolescence, but the continuing process of facing in both our external and interior worlds, times that challenge and test us. It's important here to recognise that wilderness is part of our human experience. We cannot avoid it; it is part of the fabric of what we are – which is a person not an object. So it's important that we try to make such wilderness periods creative rather than destructive. We do this, not by denying or repressing our feelings of desolation, but by looking them square in the eye, and using them as aids as we grow to full humanity.

Once we recognise all this churn, the story of Jesus in the wilderness can take on a relevance it may not have had before. Taken at face value, especially in the extended accounts in Matthew and Luke, we see someone who is presented, uniquely, as the 'Son of God' doing battle with supernatural forces, while being ministered to by equally fantastical angels. But what happens if, instead, we accept Jesus as a figure representing our own human struggle? The story of temptation by the devil takes on fresh meaning. Rather than seeing it as a supernatural assault, it can be understood as the wilderness experience of someone wrestling with his or her own psyche and conscience, and trying to plot the right course in difficult circumstances. Are there not points of recognition here for all of us?

Surely the three temptations in Luke 4:1-13 are enticements that all of us have had to struggle with – materialism, self-aggrandisement and power. In the first temptation Jesus is told to turn stones into bread to satisfy his hunger. The answer he gives is well known: 'One does not live by bread alone' – both a spiritual and a psychological truth. Human beings are more than material entities and we cannot function adequately if our lives consist of nothing more than material satisfaction.

A story is told that during the last war there were two huts of women prisoners in a Nazi extermination camp. Both were living in similar conditions, neither group had anything like enough food, clothing or warmth, and the long-term prognosis for them all was poor. Yet one hut seemed to fare better than the other. It had among its number a very old woman, too old and too weak to work, who therefore received no rations. So the others in that hut shared their meagre supplies to help keep her alive. In return, she told them stories about their traditions, their past and their country. She connected them to a purpose and a meaning in life beyond their present degradation and peril. Despite having one more mouth to feed than the neighbouring hut, these women had a better survival rate.

Human beings cannot 'live by bread alone'. If we try to, it will be to our greater impoverishment. Yet it is a question we repeatedly have to face; in ordering our priorities we can all too easily favour a quick materialistic fix rather than nourish the deeper needs of our spiritual well-being.

The next two temptations, self-aggrandisement and power, may seem to have nothing to do with 'the man (or woman) in the street', but only with those in positions of responsibility and public office. Not a bit of it. Of course, such people have more literal power, and the temptation to abuse it is there, but in truth it's a temptation that's open to each of us on a daily basis. For example, do we try to make ourselves look better at the expense of others, or do we resist? Do we treat those 'below' us on the social scale as menials unworthy of our notice, or as valued people in their own right? Do we measure our importance in terms of wealth, possessions, power and influence, or do we repose it in the value we place on the individual as a brother or sister in creation? If our self (our ego) remains at the centre of our world, then we have failed in our wilderness encounters; the 'devil' has won and we are diminished.

In times of wilderness our values and norms are challenged. They may be forced upon us by a tragic event, by physical or psychological illness, by the death of a loved one, by the loss of a job. Wilderness may even result from a happy occurrence – a marriage, a baby, moving home or finishing a degree. Wilderness is a time when our values and norms no longer measure up to the perceived reality of a situation; it is a time for taking stock, re-evaluating and perhaps changing direction. Wilderness may be a major catastrophe or a minor upset; the common factor is that such turbulence forces us into decisions about our direction in life.

For those attempting to live in the Spirit, wilderness is an opportunity to look at life, and judge it by values other than those of prevailing cultural norms. In recent times, the trend has been towards individual selfishness and self-aggrandisement. This seemed to be exemplified by the Thatcherite '80s when material excess was valued above social responsibility. For people enthused by that zeitgeist, the answer to all three of the devil's questions would have been 'Yes please'.

A crisis or traumatic event can stop us in our tracks and make us look again at such values, and grasp afresh that 'one does not live by bread alone'. But wilderness needs to be more than a series of events that may or may not happen to us throughout our lives. If we're serious about living a spiritual life, wilderness must be something we deliberately include in our regular activities. Wilderness is an attitude to life that stops us accepting a comfortable status quo, and challenges us to review our priorities and the direction we're taking.

These days, many people choose to do so through the medium of a retreat. It could be either religious or non-religious in nature. Some retreats are led, and addresses are given on a particular theme to a group; some are individually led and there's no common input; while other individuals simply choose to withdraw to a quiet spot for a few days (into their own private wilderness) to think life through at a deeper level than is usually possible.

Whatever may or may not have actually happened to Jesus, I'm sure he would have experienced, on more than one occasion, the benefits of time in the wilderness. In his place of birth (almost certainly Nazareth, not Bethlehem), and in the area of the Galilee, it would have been easy enough to find suitable wilderness areas, literally as well as metaphorically. It would have been part of his life plan to search out the truth within his own soul, and then act on the answers he perceived.

What we have in the wilderness stories related in the Gospels is a paradigm for our own spiritual journey. We, too, have to contend with the 'devils' of greed, materialism, self-aggrandisement and power. To draw insights from these stories we do not need to believe them literally. They speak metaphorically of our need for the discipline of the wilderness experience in our own lives, and the need to use creatively the times of wilderness that are thrust upon us against our will or reason. The 'devil' is an ever-present tempter in our own psyche constantly bidding us to take the easy option and live less than fully human lives.

Like the best of men and women who had gone before him, or lived after him, Jesus was a man of unalloyed integrity, willing to risk his life and go to his death rather than compromise the truth for which he stood. We are challenged by his life, and by the lives of other great men and women to reach for such a level of integrity and truth; but it is a life that is achieved only if we're willing to face our own personal demons. Nothing comes from nothing; wilderness cannot be avoided on the road to spiritual and human maturity, and the story of Jesus in the wilderness is also our story.

On the bright side, Jesus was, we are also told, ministered to by angels. As we engage with the wilderness, either of our own choosing or one that's forced upon us, we too need ministering angels. It has been my experience that, when going through wilderness experiences, there have always been 'angels' at my side ready to help pick up the pieces.

Their presence is not usually obvious. Usually they come in the guise of good friends with whom I have shared something of my journey. They are invariably down to earth, good-humoured and lavish with the gin. If you choose to enter into wilderness in a way that will enable and enhance your spiritual development, make sure you have an 'angel' or two on hand to lean on. This is not a journey we need to take alone – it is a cojective experience where heart meets heart. And at some point, when the wilderness has transformed your halo into a doughnut and coffee, and your wings into arms that embrace, you will find that you, too, are being a ministering angel to somebody else. It's all very human and, as such, very divine.

# CHAPTER 18

## Transfiguration – taking the right path

The Transfiguration of Christ is one of the most problematic 'events' in the four Gospels. It appears in the first three, Luke giving the fullest account. Let's take a look.

> 'Jesus took with him Peter and John and James, and went up on the mountain to pray. And while he was praying, the appearance of his face changed, and his clothes became dazzling white. Suddenly they saw two men, Moses and Elijah, talking to him. They appeared in glory and were speaking of his departure, which he was about to accomplish at Jerusalem. Now Peter and his companions were weighed down with sleep; but since they had stayed awake, they saw his glory and the two men who stood with him. Just as they were leaving him, Peter said to Jesus, "Master, it is good for us to be here; let us make three dwellings, one for you, one for Moses, and one for Elijah" – not knowing what he said. While he was saying this, a cloud came and overshadowed them; and they were terrified as they entered the cloud. Then from the cloud came a voice that said, "This is my Son, my Chosen; listen to him!"' (Luke 9:28-35)

What are we to make of this? Some suggest that it's a resurrection story that has somehow been 'misplaced' in the text of the Gospels. Others say it's a myth, a story inserted to make a theological point about Jesus and who he was. Yet others prefer to insist it's simply an account of what actually happened on a mountain in Judea.

Where the truth lies (and it may be a composite of all three claims) is something we can never know, but that shouldn't worry us. Our concern here isn't historical accuracy or theological correctness, but spiritual reality. What in this story gels for us today? How can we use it as a guide on our own journey towards full humanity? As with all biblical stories and myths, and those of the other great religions, if we don't make them our own in the here and now they become burdens on such a journey rather than vehicles to lighten our load.

I'm in my late sixties and obviously more than halfway through my life. So it's all down hill from here – right? As thoughts of my own mortality, my own death, grow more intrusive with every breath I take, I'm increasingly wondering – is my glass (at least) half empty, or is it almost half full? It's a vitally important question because it will determine how I conduct the rest of my life. Let's paint a picture we can all identify with. If life is a large glass of wine (or whatever takes your fancy), it is brim-full at the beginning and we drink of it freely because it's almost impossible to believe it will ever run out. But as the years pile up it becomes increasingly clear that our personal allocation of wine is indeed very limited.

How do we react? One response is denial, a popular ploy in modern western society. We pretend that death doesn't really exist, that the wine will flow without limit. Death is sanitised and an embarrassment when it's encountered. The bereaved often become social outcasts because they're a living reminder that the grim reaper awaits us all. The bereaved are allowed about two months to get over a death, after which 'normal service' is expected to resume. (In reality, a normal bereavement period will last anything from two to five years.)

The cosmetics industry and plastic surgery thrive on people who try to convince themselves that their glass will never empty. Stay young, dye your hair, smooth your wrinkles, lift your face. Yet that glass *will* empty. Now I'm no kill-joy and have no problems about people looking good and fighting to stay healthy, but vain attempts to deny the inevitable simply wastes what time/wine you have left. Where's the merit or joy in that? Consider the following thought…

A man builds his house by the river. It's a beautiful site and he looks forward to spending a long and happy life there. But over the years the river slowly changes course. His front door, originally 30 feet from the river bank, is now only 10 feet away. Rather than face the fact that he will eventually have to sacrifice his house to the river, he starts to reinforce the bank. Every spare moment is taken up with this work so he has little time for anything else. In old age his efforts cannot keep up with the demands of the river. One day, after heavy rainfall, the river bursts its banks. He dies along with his house, and there's no one to mourn the loss.

Another reaction to the dwindling wine supply is to admit the inevitable but try to conserve what's left. It's the 'I'm too old to do that sort of thing', or the 'I like things to stay as they've always been' approach. Many people, after they reach mid-life (and sometimes before), avoid the challenge of old age and death by setting their lives in aspic. Change happens only when it's forced upon them from the outside, and then it's resented and resisted. Maintaining the status quo is the name of the game, and it often masquerades positively as 'old fashioned values' or 'respect for the past'.

Again, there's nothing wrong with either attitude in itself. Much good from the past needs preserving, but when it's simply used as a block against the passing of time, it becomes a denial of life and is as neurotic as attempts to remain forever young. Like wine, life should not simply be preserved, but enjoyed to the last drop.

A variation on the last-drop technique is a third false reaction to a half-empty glass. Mid-lifers who recognise that mortality is an increasingly insistent presence, choose to down their wine with ever-greater gusto. This seems to improve on the milquetoast approaches, but may get the focus wrong – life is lived to the full but at an almost exclusively material level. Sensations are indulged, experiences are sought and energy expended in the hope it will lend meaning to an otherwise unfulfilled existence. But the active approach doesn't have to be so limited. Acts of selflessness, journeys of adventure and discovery, charitable work, can all be grasped by those wanting to invest their lives with purposeful action. So that's the choice – many will feel fulfilled while others, especially those who merely focus on their own appetites, will feel dissatisfied, or suffer a severe hangover when the wine is drunk to excess.

A fourth, what I want to call the spiritual path, is to realise that the glass is never actually empty. As the wine level drops, the space in the glass is replaced by air ('pneuma' – spirit). This approach to life moves the focus off quantity ('how much have I got left?') and onto quality ('what sort of life do I have?').

We're both physical and spiritual beings, but if we live exclusively at the physical and material level ('What do I possess? How can I get more? What time is left to me?') then no matter how much we have, we always want more – especially more time. But embrace the spiritual dimension of our lives, no matter how we express it, and we begin to see that the glass is never empty. No matter how much or how little we have in material terms, or how much or how little time we have, our glass is always full and we are free to get on with living in the here and now. There's no need to 'eat, drink and be merry, for tomorrow we die'.

Death is still the great unknown. We neither know when it will arrive, nor if anything lies beyond. Nor will it necessarily be a welcome release; the spiritual person rejoices in this life free from denial thanks to the quality of their present existence. We need only to acknowledge that death is inevitable, then get on with what we're doing.

The Transfiguration of Jesus seems to me to represent the axis point of life, when we look back over the past, assess the present, and wonder what the future will bring. This is what happens in the story: Jesus meets Moses and Elijah, who represent the law and the prophets. Over the period of his ministry, Jesus's teaching was often criticised for not being orthodox. Here, in his encounter with Moses and Elijah, he is shown to be vindicated. He, and not the institutions of his time, is shown to be the way that leads to God. Jesus's history is compared with the history of Israel, and is not found wanting.

In the light of this knowledge we are told that 'Moses and Elijah... were speaking of his departure, which he was about to accomplish at Jerusalem'. The path that Jesus had chosen was confirmed as the right one; his future would continue in the same direction and lead inevitably to his death. The voice from the cloud confirmed again that all was right with this man.

In many art works, of most religions, holy individuals are depicted with halos, or as projecting an inner radiance. In my life so far, I have met just a couple of people who, if I were to use descriptive language about them, I would say 'shone'. I don't mean they literally glowed, but there was something about them that really did seem to 'shine from the inside out'. It is something about a life lived to the full, where choices have been made that lead to a certain man or woman becoming a fully integrated personality. The story of the Transfiguration of Christ is just that, the picture of a man who is thoroughly integrated and whole. The pictorial language of the story need not put us off. In its dramatic and other-worldly way it is saying that, in the face of hard choices, in the knowledge and near presence of death, in the face of great opposition, it is still possible to make the right decisions and take the spiritual path.

At our mid-life point, we may not glow with complete integration, but neither should we despair. Our glass is only half empty if we consciously take that view. To be transfigured is to see the world from a spiritual perspective, and live it that way.

To judge Jesus in material terms is to judge him an utter failure. He had no recognisable power, no wealth and, as far as we know, no permanent home. He was killed after just three years of public life, and most of his friends deserted him. On this evidence, I certainly wouldn't make him CEO of my company! Yet despite such failure, his short life changed the world, not because he was divine in some unearthly sense, but because he taught us what it is to be a fully integrated human being. Few people even want to be so completely whole; instead we get caught up in patterns and behaviours that stop us seeing our own potential. Yet there have been, and are, people who have followed Jesus's pattern and have transfigured not only themselves but their world: St Francis of Assisi, Mahatma Gandhi, Mother Teresa of Calcutta and Nelson Mandela immediately come to mind.

Transfiguration is something we can all experience. It comes from the choices we make, where our priorities lie and the vision we have of life, both our own and life in general. It is important therefore that we do not dismiss the story of Christ's Transfiguration as a fairy tale. Nor should we simply reduce it to a historical event which did, and could only have happened to Jesus.

Transfiguration happens to us when we integrate our lives. When we prioritise the spiritual over the material we are released from the fear of death, and the quality of our lives is transformed. And it isn't even all or nothing. We're not suddenly transfigured into some new sort of being (although profound shifts of perception can lead to startling changes in a person's life). Being transfigured is a process that happens when we pursue the spiritual path, a path routed in down-to-earth good sense, love, compassion and a yearning to do the truth.

As I have already said, this type of life may be embraced in and through religion – as three of the examples above were. Yet it need not be so. We will recognise such transfigured lives wherever and however they are lived. We recognise them, not because such individuals are aware of such a qualities within themselves, but because of the effect they have on others, and sometimes because they really do seem to 'glow' from the inside out.

In the book *Dying we Live* edited by H. Kuhn Gollwitzer, he assembled a collection of letters by victims of Nazi atrocity. It reveals that under threats of violence and death some German men and women declared that they would rather be imprisoned and killed than involve themselves in the evils perpetrated by the regime. Here's just one short extract:

> A farm boy from the Sudetenland, February 3, 1944
> Dear parents,
> I must give you bad news – I have been
> condemned to death, I and Gustave G. We did not
> sign up for the SS, and so they condemned us to
> death. Both of us would rather die than stain our
> consciences with such deeds of horror. I know what
> the SS has to do... I thank you for everything you have
> done for my good since my childhood; forgive me,
> pray for me...

It isn't technology that will ultimately save our world, nor mankind's manipulation of the environment. Nor will the pious platitudes of those who place religion at the heart of our salvation deflect us from heading towards chaos and disaster. What will transform our world positively will be transfigured lives, lives like that of this Sudetenland farm boy. Each of us can choose how we live our lives. Transfiguration really is an option open to all.

In the next chapter we will explore the process by which this can happen.

# CHAPTER 19

## Death and resurrection – the process of becoming

The resurrection of Jesus has been the central proclamation of the Church since its inception. On this 'fact' alone the Church was established and from it arose the belief that Jesus was literally the Son of God. All of the Church's creeds, doctrines, dogmas and traditions, all its institutions and practices, and all that the Church is today, stem from that single belief – that Jesus rose bodily from the dead.

Yet as with other 'events' in his life, problems arise for those who insist that the resurrection story recorded in the Gospels must be taken at face value. So, first, try comparing all four Gospel accounts of the resurrection for yourself and ask yourself the following questions.

Who first discovered the empty tomb? Who were there, angels or men, and how many? To whom did Jesus first appear, and where? Was he touched or was he not?

It's quite clear from reading all four stories together that they cannot all literally be true; the 'facts' simply do not gel into one coherent story. Yet this in itself should not surprise us. The Gospels were not written down for some 30 or more years after Jesus's death, and in the telling and re-telling stories do change.

If you recall my dismal failure, in Chapter 1, to recall events shown to me only minutes before on a television screen, I think you'll agree that it must be pretty easy, after more than 30 years, for discrepancies to creep into four different texts. What we have to concede, therefore, is that we cannot know for sure exactly what did or did not happen on that first Easter day. One thing is clear, however: to insist that Jesus's actual physical body was reanimated at that time is not supported by the text. Nevertheless, it seems to me that literal belief in the bodily resurrection of Jesus is no more essential to belief in his spiritual strength than is literal belief in the virgin birth.

But that's not to dismiss the fact that something must have happened to turn 11 frightened men into bold proclaimers of Jesus's resurrection. It is hard to imagine that any contrived story about the stolen body of a religious leader could have such a world-changing effect. Nor does the often-put theory that Jesus fell into a coma on the cross, only to be revived by the cold tomb, cut any ice. Both scenarios presuppose a shameless and shameful con-trick on the part of both Jesus and/or his followers. Mighty empires come and go, so I can't credit that Christianity would have lasted almost 2000 years with nothing more to support it than a devious religious con.

So it isn't the resurrection itself I want to challenge, but the interpretation, and the religious accretions that have settled upon it over the centuries. In Chapter 11, I said that I remain agnostic about life after death, and that's still the case. None of us can know for certain whether or not 'life' survives death, and if it does, what form it takes. To judge from the available 'evidence' I believe that the probability that it does is at least as reasonable as the likelihood that it doesn't. In my agnosticism, however, I refrain from drawing any religious conclusion from the possibility.

So let's examine the resurrection of Jesus but stripped of its Christian baggage. If we consider Jesus of Nazareth to be a paradigm for unblemished humanity, it is reasonable to assume that whatever happened to him is also accessible by us, not through belief or faith, but by virtue of that common humanity. So let's ask, first, has anyone else, at any time, shared what could be called resurrection experiences? The answer clearly is: Yes. For example, in his book *The Silent Road*, Major Tudor Pole recounts this story:

> 'During the last war a company commander well known
> to me was killed by a sniper's bullet at the beginning of
> an engagement in the Palestine hill country. He was
> so loved by his men that it was decided not to disclose
> his death until the battle was over. This officer was

killed at seven in the morning and yet throughout that day he was seen leading his men into the attack and on several occasions his speech and guidance saved those under his command from ambush and probable annihilation.

'At the end of the day when the objective had been successfully reached, this officer went among his men and thanked them for their bravery and endurance. He spoke, and was spoken to in a perfectly natural way. It was only later the same night when the men were told that their commanding officer had been killed early that morning that he ceased to be visible to them and even then there were many who could not be convinced that their leader had 'gone west'. This experience I can vouch for personally as I was there, and I know of others of a similar kind.'[4]

Compare the last sentence of that quotation with the penultimate verse in St John's Gospel: **'This is the disciple who is bearing witness to these things, and who has written these things; and we know that his testimony is true.' (John 21:24)**. Both writers are claiming to have witnessed similar events, the difference lying not in the quality of the post-mortem experiences, but in the cultural conditioning of those involved. Jesus's life, teaching, death and post-mortem appearances were set in a particular religious context. There was an expectation, certainly among Jesus and his followers, that God was about to intervene in history and bring the world as they knew it to an end. It was expected that the Messiah, the Anointed One, would come and liberate the Jewish nation from its bondage (at that time under the Roman Empire).

It isn't difficult to see how the sort of event described by Tudor Pole, above, would be interpreted in 1st-century Palestine. Religious significance would be layered upon it in a way that didn't happen in 20th-century Palestine during the Second World War. It's easy to see how the Church, in the years following the post-mortem appearances of Jesus, searched through the scriptures for 'proof' of their experience from within their own religious tradition.

From dogma such as Mary's Immaculate Conception, which followed much later in the Church's history, we can see the powers

---

[4] Published by Neville Spearman (1960)

of hindsight in full flow. As early as the 2nd century, the Church had developed such notions, and arguments about the Immaculate Conception rumbled on for hundreds of years. Then, in 1708, Pope Clement XI pronounced it a Feast of Obligation, but it wasn't until the Papal Bull of 1854, 'Ineffabilis Deus', that it became official dogma of the Roman Catholic Church. It isn't events themselves that give rise to items of doctrine and dogma, but rather that developing and changing perceptions *colour* our view of past events. To repeat Kant: 'We see the world not as it is, but as we are.'

Take a modern example: at the end of the Second World War the atrocities visited on the Jewish people were unarguable. There were death camp survivors, witnesses from liberating armies, film footage and still photographs, physical remains (some preserved) of the camps, and documented evidence from the Nazis' own files. Yet some people, even now, refuse to believe any of it. They say the holocaust never happened and want to rewrite history. They hear only what they want to hear, and see only what they want to see: beliefs create 'facts', not facts create beliefs. We've been here before in this book: there are none so blind…

Now I'm not claiming any sinister intent by the early Church, or (on the whole) by later churchmen, but in their religious beliefs and expectations they clearly massaged the facts of Jesus's life as we now have them. Leave aside the interpretation the Church later put upon the resurrection appearances, and we can still appreciate that the resurrection of Jesus marked the appearance of a fully integrated human figure after his physical death. Seen this way, the resurrection accounts symbolise the end of our own human journey – possible for every human being – rather than the unique arrival of a God-become-man in whom we have to believe to achieve the same end.

The resurrection accounts understood in those terms become symbols of universal hope for the continuation of human existence, rather than grounds for the exclusive claims of one single religion. The Christian explanation of the resurrection 'event' is understandable given the historical environment in which it took place, and a legitimate interpretation for Christian believers. But, as we've also seen, more than one interpretation is valid for the 21st century.

Whatever did or did not happen on that first Easter day will have to remain a mystery – we simply cannot know. But the importance of the death and resurrection of Christ stretches far beyond historical investigations and doctrinal discussions; they represent for us the very substance of human growth and development. The truth about death and resurrection is found not in scriptural texts, but within the human psyche. At a very basic and natural level one can engage with this truth through the passage of the four seasons. In nature the birth-death-birth cycle is there for us to see even if we only have a window box in the middle of a concrete city.

Jesus often lifted analogies from nature in his parables and teaching. A sower went out to sow... Unless a seed falls into the ground and dies it remains a single grain, but if it dies it bears much fruit... Look at the flowers of the fields... The kingdom of heaven is like a grain of mustard seed... The human psyche is reflected in the physical and organic nature of the world around us. To understand this and to harmonise with it is to mature into the full flowering of our humanity, to become integrated personalities living to full capacity.

Unlike other events in the life of Jesus, his death and resurrection do not equate with any particular life stage, but are processes that encompass the whole of our human development. Birth is not possible without death. For fertilisation to progress the individual ovum and sperm 'die' to themselves in order to create an embryo and foetus. For the baby to be born it has to 'die' to its own protective environment within the womb and be pushed out into an alien world (perhaps our most traumatic experience of all). For the baby to become an infant, it has to 'die' to its need for milk alone and be born into the world of 'solids'. It's a never-ending process of physical change. Only when life stops does this process cease; we can do little to alter its natural rhythm.

If we're realistic about our physical condition it'll help us be more acutely aware of our spiritual and psychological needs. Perhaps we can do little or nothing about our physiology (medical interventions excepted), but we can do a great deal about our psyche. An acceptance of death and resurrection as a necessary and inevitable process can lead us towards creative development of the same process on a spiritual and psychological level. Science itself uses the processes of death and resurrection to advance – when a hypothesis seeks to explain certain phenomena it will hold sway until disproven or replaced by a better explanation. Only in this way do the material sciences advance. It may be a painful process for an individual scientist or a scientific community but, in pursuit of knowledge, death and resurrection, thesis and antithesis, go hand in hand.

Accepting death as a precursor to advancement – I'm speaking spiritually and psychologically here – is the key to full and creative living, to living life in its resurrected form here and now. The death of long held ideas – of ways of living, patterns of behaviour, relationship expectations, sexual stereotypes and religious beliefs – does not cease to be painful. But to change any of these things is a real psychological death, and the grief process may be profound.

Yet to avoid change, to remain ossified in the way we react to the world is equally, if not more, death-dealing. It is death-dealing for the individual because life becomes smaller and more limited, vision is narrowed and opportunities are missed or resisted. It is also death-dealing for those around us. People who become set in their ways, who avoid the pain of death, also avoid growth and being stimulated by resurrection. They also frustrate the growth of others by their fear-driven need to maintain homeostasis (same state) in their own lives.

Yet if we reflect for just a moment on both our own physical condition and the world of nature, we will see that homeostasis is unnatural – to live is to change.

If death and resurrection are nothing more than belief in a 1st-century man, we consign to the past the very process that gives us life. When I practised as a therapist and counsellor I considered my main objective to be helping others to enter into the process of death and resurrection for themselves. It's about supporting an individual's struggle to liberate himself or herself from perceptions and attitudes that limit them as people and prevent them embracing a more authentic life. Often the going is hard, tears are not infrequent and resistance can be fierce, yet we struggle on together because the alternative is worse – an inauthentic life dominated by the past. In spiritual terms, too, a person's attempts to cling onto dogmatic beliefs can be fierce. For me and for those with whom I share the spiritual journey, there is always another death to face; the journey does not end with this life, whatever the next may, or may not bring.

I have often thought of the spiritual journey as a bit like hill-walking. Sometimes it's cold and miserable, sometimes the fog descends and visibility all but disappears. There are times when, wet through and chilled to the bone, I've wanted nothing more than to retreat to a warm pub back down the valley. Yet there are other moments of clarity when the view opens up and the spectacle is breathtaking. At such times I've known that the pub wasn't really an option, for no way could it compare to the beauty and vision, the exhilaration and sense of achievement of reaching the top. But, of course, as any hill-walker knows, there is always another top, or, if the landscape or seascape is different, another horizon to discover, and the journey goes on.

When I became a Franciscan brother, part of my novitiate involved spending a number of months at the one house in the order that was a monastery rather than a friary, so life was lived mostly within the monastery walls and there was a good deal of silence. Immediately prior to this I had been assistant to the Minister Provincial, which involved a great deal of travelling around the various friaries, as well as other external engagements. The change was profound. From an active high-profile life I became the 'least of the brethren' doing everyone's washing in the laundry, and not much liking the change.

During my time in the monastery, where much time was given to prayer and silence, God disappeared. For me he simply ceased to be – he wasn't absent, just non-existent. In the 'power-house of prayer' all that I was left with was a black hole where God had once been. The pain was intense. I wept, I cursed and I went through the motions of my daily routine in dark despair. God had, for me, died; and with God went my whole reason for being both where I was and who I was.

This period of utter blackness lasted about two months (it seemed like years), but then, out of this very real experience of death, came my resurrection. It is hard to put the experience into words. The God in whom I had believed up to that point still remains dead to me, and I'm more agnostic now about most things than I ever was. Yet now I know. I do not know about God, but I know deep within my being that there is a dimension to life that has the quality of eternity – that the divine dwells in the very centre of my being. I felt, and feel, resurrected, lifted from the tomb of dogmatic belief into the 'liberty of the sons of God'. For me this was, and remains today, a profoundly human experience that I believe is open to all who seek a spiritual way of living.

By holding the death and resurrection of Jesus as its central precepts, the Christian Church is holding onto a truth that has significance for us all. This significance, however, has nothing to do with religious belief, but reveals through Jesus's example the most profound and universal laws of the universe. This process of death and resurrection is at one with the human psyche, a means through which mankind identifies fully and completely with what it is to be human. It is, to quote C S Lewis's *The Lion, the Witch and the Wardrobe*, '**the deep magic from before the dawn of time**'.

One can call the destination of such a process 'the kingdom of God' or, in Jungian terms 'individuation', or from Eastern traditions, 'enlightenment'. The name we give it is only relevant insofar as it enables or prevents people from entering into the process for themselves. The process of 'becoming' through death and resurrection is a profoundly human process. In Jesus, the Church has a magnificent icon who enables and encourages followers on their journey towards wholeness; it must accept, however, that the truth he embodies is for all, regardless of their religious affiliation or lack of it.

So don't be afraid of the pain that death brings, for in its wake comes a newness and quality of life that can truly be called resurrection. In his little book *The Prophet*, Kahlil Gibran writes: '**Your pain is the breaking of the shell that encloses your understanding.**'

Breaking the shell (or the mould) is a radical process. The spiritual life challenges both our personal norms and often those of our society. Do not set out on the path of death and resurrection if you want a quiet life; you will be called on to be as radical today as Jesus was in his time. But in dying you will live, and eternity will break in upon you, and you will never be the same again.

# CHAPTER 20

## Ascension – being who I'm meant to be

Children often produce amusing but unexpectedly penetrating insights into difficulties that can arise from a too-literal grasp of biblical phrasing. Take one mother who was mystified by her children's Bible chat. Her six-year-old was explaining to her younger child why God was not only left-handed but had little choice in the matter. Why? Simple, the child said, pointing to Mark 16:19: **'So then after the Lord had spoken unto them, he was received up into heaven, and sat on the right hand of God.'** (King James version). And in the Book of Common Prayer, the Creed states: '**… And ascended into heaven, And sitteth on the right hand of the Father.'** Result? Enforced left-handedness! But why penetrating? Read on…

The story of the Ascension comes to us from the author of Luke and The Acts of the Apostles. Matthew and John are silent on the subject, and as we can see, above, Mark's Gospel gives us little to go on, and what is there is thought to be a later addition to the original text.

St Luke's Gospel says: **'While he was blessing them, he withdrew from them and was carried up into Heaven.' (Luke 24:51)** Yet not all the early texts include '…and was carried up into heaven', so there's little in Luke to reinforce a doctrine of Jesus's Ascension.

The fullest text we have is in The Acts of the Apostles:

'When he had said this, as they were watching, he was lifted up, and a cloud took him out of their sight. While he was going and they were gazing up toward heaven, suddenly two men in white robes stood by them. They

143

said, "Men of Galilee, why do you stand looking up toward heaven? This Jesus, who has been taken up from you into heaven, will come in the same way as you saw him go into heaven.'" (Acts 1: 9-11)

We can laugh at a child's literal interpretation of Jesus 'sitting on God's right hand', yet it is only a step away from what the Church has managed to construct from very meagre texts. The Church is still wedded to the idea that the Ascension is about Jesus's vertical bodily take-off. Whatever did or didn't actually happen, I'm sure of one thing: the Ascension is not about a jet-fuelled figure disappearing into the stratosphere. Chapels dedicated to the Ascension with a pair of plaster feet sticking out of a plaster cloud in the ceiling may have once been a helpful visual aid, but it does nothing for me (except raise a smile) as we enter the third millennium AD.

So what are we to make of the Ascension? And what is its relevance today? As with most 'events' in the life of Jesus, I'm agnostic about how much reportage is historical fact and how much is the early Church's mythologising. If, as we read in the previous chapter, the resurrection appearances of Jesus were not unlike, though perhaps qualitatively different from, the post-mortem appearances described by Tudor Pole, then some sort of dematerialisation would seem to have occurred. But that is still quite some remove from bodily ascension.

If we're dealing with a mythological reading then we can see how the language of ascension would be appropriate. At a time when 'heaven' was thought to be another place, literally above the sky where God 'dwelt', then Jesus 'rising up' to share a closer relationship with God would have made sense. Ascension represents going home, a completion. It's at this point that we can identify with the story ourselves and make it our own.

Whatever we believe did or didn't happen to Jesus, the Ascension is a metaphor for our own completion of the journey – psychologically and spiritually – as human beings, and being at one with ourselves and the world around us. It's a wholeness of being which, for those who care to use such language, may be called divine. Carl Jung called this process 'individuation', the end point of the process of settling in to who we really are. In this life it seems to me that few if any individuals achieve this full state of integration or individuation. There are so many possibilities for each of us, so much potential that probably remains unfulfilled, that full integration rarely rises above possibility to become a probability in this life.

In his book *Jungian Dream Interpretations,* James Hall puts it this way:

> Individuation… refers to the process in which a person in actual life consciously attempts to understand and develop the innate individual potentialities of his or her own psyche. Because the archetypal possibilities are so vast, any particular individuation process inevitably must fail to achieve all that is innately possible. The important factor, therefore, is not the amount of achievement, *but whether the personality is being true to its own deep potentialities* rather than simply following egocentric and narcissistic tendencies or identifying with collective cultural roles. [5]

Staying true to our own deepest potentiality must be our spiritual lodestar; it's about discovering and then living out our true self. It will involve many acts of death and resurrection. It will mean searching beyond the 'little me' satisfactions which expect instant gratification, to our deeper Self which, cojectively, connects with the deepest Self in others and the very Being of the universe in which we live. When we start to transcend our own individual neurotic selves, then we begin to experience wholeness and begin to heal our personalities.

In his Tavistock Lectures, Jung writes about the healing process:

> It is an individuation process, an identification with the totality of the personality, with the self. In Christian symbolism the totality is Christ, and the healing process consists of the 'Imitatio Christi'.[6]

Jung is saying here that healing comes through identity with the *symbolism* of Christ, because the most profound moments in Christ's life, as described in the Gospels, are not available as ideal exemplars if

---

[5] Inner City Books, Toronto, (1983) (My Italics)
[6] Analytical Psychology, Routledge & Keegan Paul, London (1986)

they are treated as literal historical events. We can only imitate Christ if we interpret his whole life as a profound myth, a paradigm against which to measure our own humanity. Truly to aspire to Christ-like virtue is not to try to emulate him, for he was a particular person in a particular historical and cultural setting. Attempting such a feat is a mistake Christians have made down the ages. First, it makes the person of Jesus exclusive rather than inclusive; second, and more important, it reduces us to inauthentic living. To imitate Christ in his actions, teaching, behaviour and so forth, is to negate who *we* really are by copying someone else. It's nothing more than hero-worship, and certainly won't lead us on our own journey towards integration and wholeness.

When I was a boy my hero was Steve Reeves, a one-time Mr Universe turned film actor who starred in sword-and-sandal epics like *Hercules Unchained*. I can still conjure up the visuals in my mind – two teams of horses strapped to him and whipped to go in opposite directions, trying, vainly, to tear him apart. Steve Reeves was my hero because he was everything I was not. And when I 'rode' one of the living room chairs (my chariot), no longer was I a weedy kid picked on at school, I was Hercules, ready to take on all comers.

Hero worship, whether it's a childish dream carried into adult life, or the religiosity of a devout follower of Christ, is equally neurotic. It's about being less than we really are because it overlays another person onto what our truest self ought to be. To follow Christ productively is not to copy him, but to recognise in him a life lived as a fully authentic human being. Imitate this aspect alone and we'll embark on the road to true spirituality, integration and individuation. Only by being truly and fully ourselves can we be true to the spirit of Jesus Christ. This is the true 'Imitatio Christi'.

The Ascension of Christ represents the stage of integration that is our destiny as human beings. Because it's a process, and because it calls for constant commitment to a particular way of being and becoming, it will normally coincide with old age, the last stages of life. Yet there is nothing automatic about ascension/integration.

By the time we reach old age we've had the chance to integrate ourselves into most of life's experiences. Maybe now it's a time to reflect, a time when competition is no longer important, or less so, and when honesty, both with oneself and with others, matters more.

However, it's also clear that age isn't in itself the factor that determines an integrated personality. If I've set my life on a course of spiritual growth, cojective values and individuation, then by the time I reach old age, there's a good chance that I will have (nearly) achieved it.

If, on the other hand, the maintenance of neurotic defences and protection of my ego have become ways of life, then no matter how long I live, I'm unlikely even to approach being a fully integrated person. Old age therefore does not, automatically, ensure integration and wholeness of life; what it brings is greater opportunity. How we use that opportunity is up to us.

Similarly, a short life needn't preclude a fully integrated life – after all, Jesus was only about 33 when he died. But few of us commit to the spiritual journey as fervently as he did, so we must hope for as extended a period as possible to pull our lives into the state of completeness.

The Ascension of Christ therefore has nothing to do with supernatural aeronautics, a fantasy conclusion to an equally fantastical life. No, Ascension is the myth that represents our own journey's end. The Atonement (the pardoning and forgiveness of sins through Christ's crucifixion and resurrection) is not a doctrine in which we have to believe, but rather it's an 'at-one-ment' – our own life's goal, achievable because in Christ we see what the possibilities of a fully human life truly are.

Again, like the other 'events' in the life of Jesus, if you choose to take a more literalist view of the Ascension than I do, if plaster feet sticking out of plaster clouds symbolise something important to you, well and good. What is important is that it is your view, and not something secondhand in which you feel obliged to believe.

Whether you hold a literalist or agnostic view of the Ascension, and a mythological interpretation of its meaning, is of no great importance. What is vital to our spiritual life and therefore our humanity, is that we allow the 'event' of the Ascension to be a living fact in our lives. Only when it becomes more than an intellectual exercise or a statement of belief will it affect who we are. It's about Being – being who we are meant to be at the end of our spiritual journey, because unless we have a goal to look forward to, the journey is hardly worth starting in the first place.

# CHAPTER 21

## The pearl of great price

The theme running through this book has been one of spiritual journeying. It has taken us to places that may seem as far removed from one another as an abbey and an abattoir. Developmental psychology has rubbed shoulders with children's fairy stories, theology with popular culture, sex with prayer, and belief with disbelief.

Yet that is how it should be, because our journey is about finding our own authentic selves, becoming true to our deepest nature, and learning to live in ways that are truly fulfilling. Our search therefore is bound to take us into, and sometimes out of again, all the experiences that express our human condition. We have our being in and through our bodies, our humanity made flesh. It is in this world that we learn to discover our truest and deepest selves, yet that has to mean accepting all that we experience.

Much of what constitutes human life today is a shallow imitation of the real thing. It may offer passing pleasure or the illusion of happiness, but when spirituality is neglected there's no depth, no capacity to satisfy the profoundest desires of our human condition. Very many people, if they're honest, know this to be true. There's an emptiness to lives that crave more and more stuff if they're to feel fulfilled, so in an effort to pad out the void they pursue ever more distractions – more wealth, power, possessions or extreme activities. Or, more subtly and self-deludingly, more religion, piety and false humility. But it's all skittering over the surface. This tragic cycle continues until people only measure themselves against these external distractions; the authentic self is lost under a welter of acquired status and material stuff.

In one short parable, Jesus sums up this condition:

> 'Again, the kingdom of heaven is like a merchant in search of fine pearls; on finding one pearl of great value, he went and sold all that he had and bought it.' (Matthew 13:45)

For a long time I didn't grasp what this story was really saying. I equated the 'kingdom of heaven' with something religious, and 'selling all that he had' in a literal and materialistic way. Nothing could be further from the truth. The 'pearl of great price' is our own authentic being; it is who we have it in us to really be, and then actually be that person. It has nothing to do with being religious in itself. Although that may be the route we choose, it is not an essential one.

The route is one of spirituality as I've tried to define it in these pages. It is a human process which places at its centre the spirit that is cojectively experienced by all people. It's the spirit that looks for the good in others, it's the spirit that expresses itself in acts of love and kindness, tolerance and understanding. It is the spirit that refuses to be palmed off with shoddy imitations and glitzy counterfeits.

In the parable, the merchant sold all that he had to acquire just one pearl of great price. This is no less true for us. But the cost is much higher than just the value of our material wealth and goods, however much or little that is. The cost involved is actually 'selling' – letting go of – our old self, the persona we have carefully cultivated over the course of our lives. Many of us find that cost too high. Although in the depths of our hearts we know that life is far from satisfactory, despite perhaps enjoying great material power and wealth (or maybe because of it), we cannot face changing what has been constructed over a long period. The pain of an unsatisfactory existence seems less frightening than the thought of uncertain change. To live authentically as the human being that we most truly are, is Jesus's pearl of great price. It is a profoundly human goal that can be sought through any religion or none.

Religion can be, and often is, detrimental to the process because it buries the authority of the individual under obedience to doctrines and dogmas, which can have no authority unless they speak to the heart of the individual.

As Leslie Weatherhead wrote in his book *The Christian Agnostic*, 'the words "ought" and "believe" cannot go together'. A belief that is no more than adherence to doctrinal diktat, or the social norms of our particular society, is no belief at all. We prostitute our truest selves to our religion or social set in order to belong, in order to feel accepted. Yet it isn't our true self that is accepted, but a persona, the mask we have carefully constructed. On the outside we're one of the in-crowd; inside we're lonely, often desperate, suspecting that, 'If only they knew who I really was' or 'If only they knew what I really believed, they wouldn't like me at all'. The message of the spiritual journey is that we can indeed be our true selves, but only at the cost of jettisoning our fearful persona – a carapace we're well rid of.

This is my second attempt to write this final chapter. In the first draft I said that I wasn't out to convert anybody. I said that if you, the reader, didn't like what I had to say, never mind, cast it aside. After Ruth read it she said I was being dishonest, that I did want to convert people and that I'd be sorry if people did just dismiss me, which of course is true. I suppose what I hope this book might do is facilitate change. When I say that I don't want to convert anyone, what I'm saying is that my 'doctrine' should not be adhered to or gifted any more or less respect than any other 'doctrine', religious or secular.

If you 'believe' anything written in these pages, and if that belief eventually influences how you conduct your life, let it be because it resonates within you, because it 'connects' with what is most authentic in you. In that sense it is an offering. But if it doesn't resonate within you, if something of my truth doesn't connect with something of your truth, then please lay it aside. Spiritual truths can never be forced on anyone, only offered. And the one doing the offering (of his or her own truth) does so with a certain tone, particular use of language, and from a particular psychological, historical and cultural perspective. So it won't suit everybody.

My sincerest hope is that if, in some small way, this book can release in you a cojective view of spirituality, a lessening of barriers between religious and non-religious understanding, and between religions of different understanding, it will have served its purpose. Nothing here is argued with any insistence on finality or objectivity.

For me there always needs to be an element of the provisional, a sense that tomorrow, next week, next year, will bring new insights, new ways of understanding myself and the world in which I feel privileged to live. It is, of course, an unsettling place to be – the land of the provisional and unfinished – yet it is also exciting, stimulating and fun.

Setting out on the spiritual journey needs, to begin with, only small acts, small changes in perception, that then begin to affect who we are. For spirituality is chiefly about changing ourselves, finding our own 'pearl of great price'. Believe it or not but I am, at heart, optimistic about humanity and about the world.

Although we live in times that seem to surround us with unequalled violence and upset, I believe that women and men, deep down, are blessed with a goodness into which we can all tap. We do not have to be victims – of our past, of other individuals, or of society. No matter how deplorable our situation (unless we are mentally incapacitated), we can make choices that improve both our lot and the lot of those around us.

Making even small, seemingly insignificant, choices can begin to effect a change, the consequences of which we may never know. Small acts of kindness such as smiling and saying 'thank you' to the ticket collector or newspaper vendor can make all the difference – to us, if not to them.

When I was a Franciscan brother I hitch-hiked all over Britain. Needless to say, only one in several hundred cars ever stopped to pick me up. This was sometimes quite depressing, especially when the weather was cold and wet, but one piece of advice kept me in good fettle: 'Whenever a car passes you, give the driver a blessing.' The drivers knew nothing of my gesture, so its effect on them can hardly be contemplated, but the effect on me was noticeable. It somehow kept me operating at a level that went far deeper than the discomfort of a wet roadside vigil. It helped me to transcend my 'outer self' and find a peace that the situation did not warrant. When we 'look to the good', and give a blessing not a curse, and take the time to connect with people at a human and humane level, we begin to change our own inner world, and begin to affect the world for the better.

These small acts and thoughts may seem no more significant than spitting in the ocean, but repeated often enough by individuals they will transform their lives; repeated often enough by millions of people and the world might be changed.

To set forth and engage in the spiritual journey is to want to change ourselves for the better as human beings. It is to want to have a positive effect on the world. It is to recognise and respect the uniqueness of each individual's path, so that we never deny another person's truth. Certainly we can note that their truth is not our truth, but we must take great care before suggesting that our truth ought to be their truth.

In his book on Transactional Analysis, *I'm OK – You're OK*, Thomas Harris wrote:

> It takes only one generation for a good thing to become a bad thing, for an inference about an experience to become a dogma.
>
> Dogma is the enemy of truth and the enemy of persons. Dogma says, 'Do not think! Be less than a person.' The ideas enshrined in dogma may include good and wise ideas, but the dogma is bad in itself because it is accepted as good without examination.[7]

We must avoid dogma in both institutions and ourselves (he says dogmatically) because it does not allow the individual an authentic expression of what is true for them. Jesus never tried to 'convert' anyone to a belief system or code of laws; rather he loved them for who they were and where they were. In so doing he enabled them to respond from the depths of their own sometimes very damaged beings, and to begin the process of becoming whole and integrated.

What was good enough for such a man as Jesus (free from any Christian preconceptions about his nature) is good enough for me. In the final analysis, I believe we are called on to love. Loving is no easy task, it takes a great deal of hard work, perseverance, tolerance and discipline. It demands that we really get to know ourselves, our deepest motivations, the parts that even certain lagers cannot reach. It also demands that we remain agnostic about a good many things.

If we're religious, we need to acknowledge that our particular religion may reflect something of the truth, but certainly not all of it, and that which it does reflect may, over the years, have become tarnished and less than perfect. If we're not religious, we need to acknowledge that

---

[7] Pan Books, London (1973)

there is perhaps hidden wisdom within such doctrines that reflects our human struggle towards integration and wholeness.

To dismiss religion thoughtlessly is to judge it at a level that probably owes more to a kindergarten understanding than to a serious study of the literature or practice within any given denomination. I grow more and more agnostic as the years go by, and this progression somehow seems to sit comfortably with my humanity. I'm beginning to see that knowing about or being sure of any *thing*, does not really matter at all, even if that *thing* is my religious belief. What matters, what really counts, is that I learn to be fully me, a person who can relate to others at the deepest levels of our being. So often it has been my experience that religion actually inhibits this person-to-person interaction. It has got in the way because beliefs have been considered more important than my flesh-and-blood brother or sister with whom I've been talking.

Spiritual paths may claim many different banners or none, but what is common to them all is a sense of purpose, a discipline that is not satisfied with inauthentic living, and a concern for our fellow creatures – at all levels of the created order.

In his wonderful little modern myth *Jonathan Livingston Seagull*, Richard Bach put his finger on the pulse of spirituality. Jonathan has just 'died', and is learning on a new plane of being with the elder gull, Chiang...

> 'We can start working with time if you wish,' Chiang said, 'till you can fly the past and the future. And then you will be ready to begin the most difficult, the most powerful, the most fun of all. You will be ready to begin to fly up and know the meaning of kindness and of love.'

Those two concepts, kindness and love, have been sentimentalised and devalued in our modern world, but both require a strength of will and a steadfastness of purpose that is unmatched by any materialistic discipline known to humanity. Perhaps that is why traditional religion is such a popular alternative because – like a travel programme on television – it offers the prospect of the journey without ever having to leave your seat.

The spiritual journey helps us to become, fully, who we have it in us to be; it introduces us to a way of life that offers each of us the highest degree of satisfaction and the greatest hope for the future of our planet. Now is the time to discard the clutter that binds us to limited horizons, and separates one human being from another. Let go of your security blanket and throw your caution to the spiritual wind. The adventure is just beginning, the journey is yours, and the goal is integration and wholeness of being.

In a previous chapter I used the word 'Jihad'. As I write, Jihad has become identified with dogma-inspired violent extremism and some of the most barbaric acts, stripped of all humanity and cojective spirituality, witnessed so far in this century. But true Jihad, what is known in Islam as the Greater Jihad, is concerned with inner discipline, rooting out everything in the believer's life that is sinful and rebellious to the ways of God. If fighting is deemed necessary to protect the community against oppression, this is known as the Lesser Jihad. But within Islam, from the earliest centuries, strict codes were put in place to protect women, children, the elderly and non-combatants. What we are seeing today is not Jihad at all, but simply violence without restraint, and that is anathema to true Islam.

True Jihad, the Greater Jihad, is a spiritual path of inner conversion towards interior peace and integration. Those of us outside the Muslim community must not be deceived into thinking that Islam advocates violence. It does not. Jihad has been hijacked by political and religious zealotry, and young men, ignorant of the meaning of true Jihad, are being exploited on a daily basis. The Greater Jihad is a spiritual inner journey towards 'love and kindness', which requires a great deal more discipline and commitment than violent action.

The spiritual life, then, is about cleaving lightly to belief systems, and favouring those that deal in compassion. It also calls on us to live with an integrity that often challenges the norms of our society and confronts some of the values that are currently widely admired. Trying to live the spiritual life will undoubtedly lead you into some pretty tight spots, where religion or materialism may seem to be your only alternatives. But don't despair, look for someone who is even deeper in the mire than you are and help to pull them out. That should put both of you back on the road.

So here we are, drawing our thoughts to a close. I feel that my entire argument could be neatly summarised as: 'Be loving and practise kindness – but with backbone.' That is the essence of the spiritual life, the essence of what it is to be truly human. We need make it no more complicated than that, because if we do we only erect walls that divide. Let your love build bridges, and your acts of kindness be the means by which you communicate with your fellow travellers, for nothing makes life so worth living as the cojective bond that forms between people 'on the road'.

What's more, all that I'm asking you to consider isn't even so very new. More than 200 years ago, in his poem *The Divine Image*, that Christian mystic and deeply humane English poet William Blake taught us how to connect with the humanity and spirituality that breathes life into all true religion. He defined his God in verses that we can all understand:

> *To Mercy, Pity, Peace, and Love*
> *All pray in their distress;*
> *And to these virtues of delight*
> *Return their thankfulness.*
>
> *For Mercy, Pity, Peace, and Love*
> *Is God, our father dear,*
> *And Mercy, Pity, Peace, and Love*
> *Is Man, his child and care.*
>
> *For Mercy has a human heart,*
> *Pity a human face,*
> *And Love, the human form divine,*
> *And Peace, the human dress.*
>
> *Then every man, of every clime,*
> *That prays in his distress,*
> *Prays to the human form divine,*
> *Love, Mercy, Pity, Peace.*
>
> *And all must love the human form,*
> *In heathen, Turk, or Jew;*
> *Where Mercy, Love, and Pity dwell*
> *There God is dwelling too.*

# About the author

Chris Scott has worked as a psychologist, trainer, counsellor, psychotherapist and organisational consultant. For more than thirty years he has also been an ordained Anglican priest working in both parishes and chaplaincy. Chris is particularly interested in the interface between religion and psychology, especially those areas which enhance human well-being. In the 1970s he spent some time as a Franciscan monk. He is married to writer and broadcaster Ruth Scott; they have two grown-up children and live in west London.

www.goodbyetogod.co.uk

Lightning Source UK Ltd.
Milton Keynes UK
UKOW02f0828100516

273942UK00005B/220/P